The Demonic Wars - Winning Our Lives Back

&

Regaining Ground

~~~~~~~~

Being Demonized - The Hard Fight

&

Learning The Long Term Strategic Battle Plan

Table of Contents

What Others Are Saying

I would like to call this testimonial "Resistance to the Truth." That's where I was: a state of being that had allowed me to become demonically infested. It is the opposite of faith, which is the possession of the truth as a substance (Heb. 11:1).

Ray Gano is a man of God, whose simple method of getting to know Jesus is actually a healing and deliverance 'miracle machine.' For me, it was getting to know the Father's love through journaling, and going deeper in the Word, that set me free, all at Ray's encouragement. It works. Here is a prayer I wrote to the Father in my journal that I hope will reveal my gratitude to the Lord and His servant, Ray, for all they have done for me:

"Father, thank You for using Ray Gano to reconnect me with Your Word, which is the truth. The truth always sets us free and makes our spiritual eyes to see. This faith is the shield against the enemies of our souls. Thank You, Father, for setting me free. Thank You, Father, for using Ray Gano's ministry."

Daniel – New York, USA

I met Mr. Ray Gano in 2016. At the time, he and his wife were living in Panama and preparing to move back to the United States. I was drawn to Ray for his deep understanding of preparing for the times ahead. I was pleasantly surprised to learn just how much more Ray was really all about.

What I came to discover was that Ray was not only a strong warrior for Christ, but that he had chosen to focus on something many shy away from, perhaps even run from, as his calling to serve The Lord. Not many men are willing to tackle Satan the way Ray has chosen to take him on. Ray gets up close and personal helping people fight the demonic and his deliverance ministry is second to none. He has helped hundreds that I personally know of either rid themselves of their own demons, the demons of family members, or have a plan in place to defend against the demonic attacks that we all face at one time or another. His teachings are life changing and his patience is endless.

In my journey to serve Christ as the Co-Founder of Hear the Watchmen, I have had the pleasure of meeting many well-known men and women of today's Prophecy movement. Having said that, I have yet to meet anyone who is as dedicated as Ray in fighting the demonic oppression and saving individuals and families from the grip of Satan.

I highly recommend that you not only purchase this book, but as a carpenter would never leave home without a hammer, I hope that you make this book a part of your daily tool box as you continue your walk with Jesus.

Mike Kerr
Co-Founder
Hear the Watchmen Ministries
www.HearTheWatchmen.com

I guess I always had a vague belief in demons, but I never really thought much about them affecting my life. Demons were mostly Hollywood, or maybe for Satanists in faraway places. Definitely not something an average guy like me would ever encounter in a thousand years.

My wife and I have been married 13 years. It never occurred to me she could have a demon problem since childhood. Kathy started a downhill health spiral with fibromyalgia about a dozen years ago. We were Christians and sought prayer and healing in church. As the disease became worse and worse, we went to healing crusades in several states, all at no avail. She became totally disabled in 2008. No one ever suggested Kathy might need deliverance.

We never gave up, at least not completely. I began to feel Kathy needed help, more in a spiritual way than in a physical way. Still I never considered her to be demonized. After all, she was a Christian.

Last fall, I stumbled across some of Ray's web articles about demons. I now believe the Holy Spirit led me to Ray and I sent him an e-mail. In short, a month later I took a week off of work and with Ray's help from afar, my wife was delivered of all her demons (and fibromyalgia). Ray gave me the information I needed to lead my wife in deliverance through the power of Jesus.

Even with all of those healing crusade trips and anointed and powerful prayers, still the whole time we were ignorant of what is now the obvious. Jesus has given us the anointing power to eradicate these devils from our lives. Yet, most Christians in the church are totally missing the obvious. What a travesty. Praise God Ray Gano is on a mission to bring the church back to the basics.

I can tell you demons have no power at all against an anointed child of God that understands the power available to us in Christ. My eyes are now opened to this and I want to be a part of the solution. Like Jesus said, "my people are destroyed for a lack of knowledge".

Don E. – Tennessee, USA

I had been asking myself this question, "Can a Christian have a demon?" So, within a four-year period two different pastors had answered me "NO" but my gut told me differently. I needed help and everything I had tried wasn't working.

Then my beloved husband who had been there for me no matter what, when most men at this point would have literally given up, kept looking for an answer to help his wife. I had been battling these sicknesses for 13 years, and all of my diseases had no cure.

A few of the diseases that I had been diagnosed with included:

- Fibromyalgia
- Neuropathy
- Degenerative Disc
- Osteoarthritis

The one disease that my pain management doctor focused on was Fibromyalgia. The pain was unbearable most of the time. I had lost all hope to go a day without pain, and pain medication.

My husband is a very persistent man and he was determined to find the answer for me. So, if someone is diagnosed with something that is incurable, then it's from the enemy, and he has studied spiritual warfare for years. We had been to many conferences, and he read lots of books on spiritual warfare. Then, as he was searching the internet one evening, he ran across information regarding deliverance from demons and many articles by Ray Gano. He knew of Ray from previous teachings, but not on deliverance. After reading more of Ray's articles, he reached out to Ray. After my husband received more information from Ray, he explained to me about their conversations and text regarding spiritual warfare.

So, as a married couple we prayed about it…a lot. I was going to have to talk about and give a lot of answers regarding very uncomfortable and personal questions. Some questions I was uncomfortable even asking myself.

As I prayed and pondered on this, I had a feeling and a conviction that came over me. I kept asking myself this question "Can a Christian have demons?" Here was someone telling me YES and he was helping others get rid of them as well.

I said to my husband and myself; "Ok, let's do this."

Believe me when I say "I would have never believed this story if it hadn't happened to me."

So, yes, I answered all of the uncomfortable questions set before me and I answered them to the best of my ability. If I hadn't answered the questions honestly, then it would have been a waste of time for Ray, my husband and myself. It wasn't easy, but that's how it works. I wouldn't have experienced deliverance and such a powerful breakthrough, plus, I would be miserable both physically and mentally. To be honest I was slowly dying.

It looks like my question "can a Christian have a demon?" was clearly answered. YES we can! And we can have more than one.

As you will read in Ray's book "a person going through deliverance when a demon is being cast out, can manifest in many different forms". So, be prayed up and ready for battle. I'm not saying this whole process is easy, because it's not. I am blessed to have a husband that honestly had no fear in him when we started this journey. Because what he saw coming out of his wife during our long nights of deliverance was not a pretty sight.

I have taken over my own deliverance. I have no fear. Any demon that was left in me had to know that I was in charge and Jesus Christ had given me the authority.

Kathy E. Tennessee, USA

I first discovered Ray Gano while watching the Branson conference back in 2012. My husband and I both found what he had to say fascinating. We bought a copy of his book, "Surviving the Coming Storm" and found the information insightful.

My husband, Josh and I, met Ray for the first-time face to face in 2016 and quickly became good friends with him. Josh and I have interviewed Ray on "Into the Multiverse" many times and it's always a pleasure to have him join us on set. We enjoy his research immensely and this new book is equally impressive!

Christina Peck
SkywatchTV

Ray Gano was mine and my daughter's main spiritual support, as well as, emotional support during the afflictions, trials, and battles we were facing at that time.

Through some of my mutual friends, posting an article on demon manifestations by Ray Gano, I was quick to seek him out for guidance. He instructed us on how to do a process of repentance and confession, and with consecrating a homemade recipe for anointing oil to be symbolic of the power of Jesus and the aroma to remind us of the Holy Spirit's presence.

Ray reminded us of the victory, and the authority that belongs to us as children of God, and that we are seated with him far above all the dark powers of Satan and his demons.

On the days when I was weary, he prayed for us and reminded us to be persistent in rebuking, repenting, and keeping on the full armor of God every day. His instruction on prayer, support, encouragement, and spiritual guidance, was a blessing from Jesus. Words will never express how much of a difference it has made on our journey of healing and deliverance.

Today, my daughter has been delivered from numerous demons that infested her as a result of abuse that then led to more sin and satanic ritual abuse. She still has a way to go in her spiritual walk. More healing and more deliverance is on its way in God's timing.

Our Faith has increased multitudes since the beginning. We give thanks to Jesus for providing Ray Gano as a counselor in our trials.

Demonic manifestations are very real and increasing in these end times. We need more people like Ray Gano to guide us to biblical truths, to encourage us to walk obedient to Jesus, to assure us that our sins are forgiven, that we are covered by the blood of the Lamb, and to be reminded to submit to God, resist the devil and he will flee from us.

Ray still keeps in touch to check on us and monitor progress. Blessings are prayed to be showered on his ministry and life for all the wonderful guidance he offers to those who still need deliverance. My daughter and I pray that he can aid others in life as much as he has in ours for the future.

Teresa S – Nevada USA

Demonic oppression is a reality and is increasing in these last days. Demons do steal, kill and destroy.

How many leaders' ministries and marriages are destroyed through sin?

As Gano writes, "Deliverance is not playing the exorcist. It is a willful act of abandoning the very lifestyle that has allowed these influences to take up residence in your life."

Even though I was involved in healing and deliverance ministry for years, I was afflicted by Fibromyalgia. The Lord revealed to me it was a demon! Once cast out, all symptoms left. Hallelujah!

It's a myth to assume ministers can't have demonic issues. So, if you are in ministry, this book is for you too.

The Father loves us so much, He longs for us to be whole and freed from all demonic oppression. Christ died on the cross for our full freedom.

Why do I trust this Battle Plan of Ray Gano's? I've followed the same biblical principles to gain deliverance in my own life and when ministering deliverance to others. Ray uses simple terms and examples. He emphasizes deliverance is an ongoing process of renewing the mind with scripture, replacing toxic thoughts and habits with godly ones, and not merely having the demons cast out.

He reminds us victory remains as we consistently crucify the sinful flesh while walking in holiness and in the spirit.

Laura Maxwell
Former Spiritualist
Radio Host on Eternal Radio
Our Spiritual Quest – http://ourspiritualquest.com

PART 1

Introduction

You are at your wits end. You may feel like you have given up on God, or God has given up on you. You have felt isolated and lost, you no longer feel like the person you once were. Your thoughts have become dark. You go to the same dark places and you spiral. You start allowing negative people and negative thoughts to influence your self-worth. Each attack pushing you closer to a precipice edge. Then, perhaps you begin to feel worthless. Hopelessness leads to a despair so grave that you look over the edge and contemplate, life is not worth living anymore.

Know that I hear and understand what you are going through. I have helped a number of people work through their deliverance and they have seen complete healing and restoration.

The first thing that I want you to understand is this- I WILL NOT JUDGE YOU! You might feel at times that I am while going through this process, but I will not. What I will do, is present pretty hard truths and at times, it's hard for people to swallow the hard truth. Especially when they have hundreds of voices in their head telling them otherwise.

This manual is a work of love. Both from a coaching side and from the receiving side.

The first thing is going to my list of questions that will help to better assess what is going on. Some of the questions are going to be rather blunt and very private in nature. But they are questions that you need to answer, and answer with as much detail as possible.

There is an old saying… "The devil is in the details."

And he does a great job hiding there. If you do not expose the details, you will not expose the devils that are living inside you.

If everything I am saying here sounds familiar, then there is a very good chance that you are what is commonly referred to as "Being demonized" another way to say that is "You have a demon infestation problem."

I have helped people get free and the program / process has been successful in helping people be free of their demons.

Be of good cheer,

Ray Gano
http://raygano.com

Needing Deliverance- Being Demonized

WARNINGS

- Deliverance is NOT a sprint, it's a marathon that you fight daily.

- Deliverance is not playing the exorcist. It is a willful act of abandoning the very lifestyle that has allowed these influences to take up residence in your life.

- Deliverance is for the desperate, for only the desperate are truly wanting to be rid of their demons. If you are not desperate enough, you will end up hanging on to some of your demons because you love them more than you love your freedom that Christ offers. Hard words, but they are the truth and YOU must make that choice.

- If you fall, immediately get right back up and continue the fight. Go back to the basics that you will learn in this battle manual. Self-pity, giving up, throwing in the towel or not believing this program works is exactly what the demons wants you to think. If you listen, you will not be free of your demons. Their goal is to steal and destroy and they ultimately want to kill YOU.

- Your first two weeks will be the toughest. By the end of the first two weeks you should be rid of most of your demons. After that, you will be in a very vulnerable state where the next 90 days the enemy will try to hit you with everything they have. You need to be ready for it. It is at this time where I see people fall and go back to their demons.

Chapter 1 - Born Again Cannot Be Demon Possessed

I am going to state it loud and clear, a true "born again" Christian cannot become demonically possessed.

NOW… "born again" Christians CAN be demonically influenced, oppressed and depressed.

I have gotten a number of emails from people who are Christians and yet claim to be "possessed."

The problem lies in the wording and yes, splitting hairs here, but in this case, I think it is important to spilt hairs because this also has a lot to do with eternal salvation and eternal security.

Problem – People use the word "possessed" as an umbrella statement.

In responding to the many emails I've received, where people claim to be "possessed", they are in reality demonically influenced, oppressed and / or depressed.

Here is the definition of Possessed…

> pos·sessed
> pəˈzest/
> adjective
>   (of a person) completely controlled by an evil spirit.
> To be possessed, a demon must "possess" that person.

If one is born again then a demon cannot "possess" that person.
Here, let's define Possess…

pos·sess

pəˈzes/

verb

have as belonging to one; to own.

IF we are "born again" then we are now owned by the Father. Nothing can pluck us from His hand and nothing can separate us from God.

We read in John 10:27 – 29…

John 10:27 – 29
27 My sheep hear my voice, and I know them, and they follow me:
28 And I give unto them eternal life; and they shall never perish, neither shall any [man] pluck them out of my hand.
29 My Father, which gave [them] me, is greater than all; and no [man] is able to pluck [them] out of my Father's hand.

To back up John 10 we read in Romans 8 that nothing can separate us from God.

Romans 8:39 "Nor height, nor depth, nor any other creature, shall be able to separate us from the love of God, which is in Christ Jesus our Lord."

This is basically the doctrine of eternal security. Once we are a child of God, there is nothing that can possess us, own us, separate us from God nor pluck us from God's hand.

Here is a simple exercise that can help drive this idea home.

Look at your left hand and say you have a black permanent marker. Write the word "ME" in the middle of your left hand.

Do it slowly and make it very clear and legible.

It should look something like this…

Let's imagine that my hand / your hand (if you are doing this exercise) is the hand of God.

The "ME" is in the hand of God and there is nothing that can pluck it out. Because it is permanent ink, it has fused with the skin of my hand and the "ME" has become part of my hand.

Now, punch the "ME" in your left hand. You can pour water on it, stab at it with your pen, and do all kinds of things to it. No matter what, you cannot separate the "ME" from the hand of God.

Note also... the "ME" cannot voluntarily leave the hand nor can the "ME" separate itself from the hand. The "ME" is part of the hand. In fact, can that "ME" do anything at all? No, it cannot. Once in the hand of God, there is nothing that "ME" can do.

I know that this is kind of a simplistic way of explaining this, but it has seemed to work in other situations when I am trying to explain the doctrine of eternal security.

SO... if the "ME" is in the hand of God, can a demon come along and possess the "ME"?

No, it can't because nothing can separate "ME" from God because it is God who now possesses me.

This means that once we are a Child of God and He possesses us, we are forever His.

A really great author William McDonald put it in very simple terms...

> "No one else can pluck them away, but a believer himself can do it" This is bizarre – that a true Christian has more power than anyone else in the universe. No one – and that includes the sheep – can remove himself from the Shepherd's strong grip... In view of such marvelous assurance, it is perverse that people should object that a true sheep of Christ should decide that he doesn't want to be a sheep any longer and could thus remove himself from his Father's hand. The argument will not stand. The words "no one" are absolute. They do not allow for any exception. The inspired text does not say "no one except a sheep of Christ himself"

In one of my email correspondence one person asked (when I was using the "ME" analogy) "We cannot be snatched out of his hand, but can we decide to leave?"

This is a great question and believe it or not, this idea is believed by many and many believe it is an aspect of "Freewill".

To answer that question, one first has to ask, would a truly born-again believer ever want to lose his / her salvation?

And second, if for some strange reason a person did want "to leave", where could they go to get away from the one who now indwells them until the day of redemption?

I personally do not believe that a true born-again believer would ever "want to leave" or lose their salvation. The key is "truly born again."

The fruit of true salvation is shown by the fact that they do persevere to the end as spoken of by Paul. This does not mean that there are not times of doubt, or even backsliding in the life of a true believer. All of us have seriously backslidden before, but we never fell out of the "hand of God."

God does not stop working in the lives of such people and the Holy Spirit does not leave them. This is actually part of the Doctrine of Regeneration, God working from within to change us from the inside out.

He continues to work to bring them back to Himself.

A person once asked a famous theologian "and what if we turn our back on God's light?" Their response … "then God's light will shine on your back."

What we need to remember is that God is faithful and doesn't give up on those that are His. AND… this is why truly born-again Christians cannot be demon possessed.

We are bought with a high price, the blood of Christ. When we come to that point in our lives where we give our lives to The Lord, He cleanses us with the blood of Christ and we are then, blood bought souls. We become "new creatures" in Christ and never again are we the filthy pig that we once were.

Charles Spurgeon stated the following…

"The man who is born for heaven hath not lifted up his soul unto vanity." All men have their joys, by which their souls are lifted up; the worldling lifts up his soul in carnal delights, which are mere empty vanities; but the saint loves more substantial things; like Jehoshaphat, he is lifted up in the ways of the Lord. He who is content with husks, will be reckoned with the swine. Does the world satisfy thee? Then thou hast thy reward and portion in this life; make much of it, for thou shalt know no other joy."

I guess the next question that you may be asking in your head, is "Am I truly saved?"

What distinguishes a true Christian from a C.I.N.O.? (Christian In Name Only)

In most cases the answer is one word – guilt. Those who are truly Christians are convicted when they sin and feel guilt whenever they do sin (and we all sin).

Those who aren't true Christians don't feel guilt, either because they have quenched the Holy Spirit or because they were never saved in the first place.

If fact, one of the sure ways to find out if you are really saved is how you react to sin. If you just shrug it off and say, "everyone sins". Then you have problems.

If you hate every sin you have committed and feel guilt every time, you are saved.

If you are a saved, born again, blood bought soul, you are a child of God. You are forever in the Hand of God, never to be plucked out by any man or anything. Nothing can separate us from God once we are one of His.

So again, based on what we have reviewed here we can clearly see that a born-again Christian CANNOT become demon possessed.

To be possessed, one has to be "owned" and we who are children of God are "owned" by God, therefore HE possesses us and we are possessed by God in the form of the Holy Spirit. It is love at the speed of light, the moment we say "YES LORD… I submit my life to You." The Holy Spirit comes in and "indwells us" possesses us and never leaves.

I hope that this little study in regard to the Doctrine of Eternal Security has helped.

Chapter 2 - How The Demonic Gains Access To One's Life & Home – What We Can Do About It

I clearly showed that Christians can NOT be possessed by a demonic / evil spirit.

But I have also shown that although we cannot be possessed, we can be oppressed, influenced, depressed, tempted, and induced and so on.

I have had a few emails asking me about how we get evil spirits / demons in our home. What people need to realize is that many Christians out there are opening themselves up to demonic oppression and do not realize it.

What Is Demonic Oppression?

Demonic oppression is an attack that result in illness, depression, excessive fear, anxiety, worry, and these things can lead to higher stressful life, broken marriages and even financial difficulty.

What we need to understand is, what are some of the things that will bring a demon into your home, and what are the things that open your home up to the evil?

How The Demonic Gains Access To One's Life & Home

Television – In today's world, television is probably the biggest influence that opens up gateways into your home.

Look at all the shows that promote evil, witchcraft, and Satanism, there was even a show titled Lucifer.

Here is what Wikipedia says about the show…

> "The series focuses on Lucifer Morningstar, the Devil, who is bored and unhappy as the Lord of Hell and resigns his throne and abandons his kingdom for the beauty of Los Angeles. Lucifer runs a nightclub in Los Angeles called "Lux", with the assistance of his demonic ally Mazikeen. Lucifer becomes involved with the LAPD when he begins to assist Detective Chloe Decker in crime cases."

Wow… Satan – bar owner and crime fighter, that is a new one.

What this is doing is desensitizing people to the demonic evil that a lot of television promotes today.

Another thing that seems to open up gateways into the home are all the shows dealing with death, murder and true crime. Again, this desensitizes the person to the actuality of death.

We need to remember that demons and the demonic wish to steal, kill and destroy.

But with shows like this we are "romanticized" and our guard drops thinking that "Satan ain't such a bad guy after all. AND HEY… he's a crime fighter to boot."

Yeah, right.

Giving Access To Our Children

I am surprised at how many children's shows promote witches, magic, the spirit realm, monsters, ghouls and other evil things as "good."

I was particularly surprised to see a popular cartoon show called "Yo-kai Watch".   Here is how it is described by Wikipedia…

> "One day while searching for insects in the woods near the town of Springdale, Arkansas, a boy named Nate comes across a peculiar capsule machine next to a "sacred tree". When he opens one of the capsules up, it brings forth the ghostly Yo-kai Whisper who gives Nate a special device known as the Yo-kai Watch. Using this, Nate is able to identify and see various different Yo-kai (spirits) that are haunting people and causing mischief. Joined by the cat Yo-kai Jibanya (a spirit cat), Nate and Whisper start befriending all sorts of Yo-kai ("good" spirits) which Nate can summon to battle against more ill-intentioned Yo-kai ("bad" spirits) that happen to live in his town, causing terrible trouble. He also goes on adventures around the town with his Yo-kai (spirit) partners to help his human friends Bear, Eddie, and Katie deal with their various problems often caused by other Yo-kai (spirits)"

This is just one show geared towards children that openly promote calling forth spirits, which there is no such thing as a "good spirit" or "bad spirit." There is evil and really evil and really REALLY evil spirits. All spirits are evil, all of them. As I have stated in writings past a demon's job is, one thing and one thing only, and that is to rob, steal, kill and destroy people.

Television Associated Products Based on These Sort of Shows

It is amazing to walk into Walmart and see many of the products associated with television shows that, promote evil, witchcraft, and the demonic.

I was walking through the toy department and was amazed at how many occult related toys and such that are being pushed on children. What is amazing is how many of these are promoted to young girls. There are toy kits that teach young girls how to become a witch, even spell books are being promoted to girls around 8 – 10 years old. I even saw pink "friendly decorated" Ouija boards that had the pointer shaped in a pretty heart.

If that isn't bad enough there was an entire section for Yo-Kai Watch and yes, you could buy your child their own watch that can help capture, control and play with your own Yo-Kai spirits. Where Pokémon is contained in balls, Yo-Kai seem to be contained in these "medals" that you can slip into the watch and use to control and pit spirits against spirits.

This is just what is being promoted to young kids. Go to Barnes & Noble and you will find a plethora of magic wands, spell books, and other magical items from the Harry Potter movies. Still to young?

What about collector figures from your favorite horror & occult movie as well as board games, books, and other "collectables" that promote evil and the occult. And that is just at a local book store.

There are many other stores that are promoting tarot cards, astrology, séances, necromancy (contacting the dead), and divination.

All these things open up your home to the evil, the demonic and create "gateways / portals" into your home which evil spirits and demons will use to gain access to your home.

This is why Television is such a huge influence for evil to enter your home, not only through the TV shows themselves, but all the products associated to these evil and occult driven television shows.

One of the best-known stories about how demons use these sort of inanimate objects as portals or gateways is the story about Annabelle a demon possessed doll.

Here is a brief story about Ed and Lorraine Warren who's "ministry" (they were catholic) was about dealing with these sort of things, and both were self-proclaimed "demonologists"….

"According to claims originating from Ed and Lorraine Warren, a student nurse was given the Raggedy Ann doll in 1970, but after the doll behaved strangely, a psychic medium told the student the doll was inhabited by the spirit of a dead girl named "Annabelle Higgins".

Supposedly, the student nurse and her roommate first tried to accept and nurture the spirit-possessed doll, but eventually became frightened by the doll's malicious behavior and contacted the Warrens, who removed the doll to their museum after pronouncing it "demonically possessed".

Source – https://en.wikipedia.org/wiki/Annabelle_(doll)

Pornography – Along the same lines where demonics enter the home is through pornography. Lust that can easily open a person up to evil spirits. In fact, there are demons who are called Incubus (male for females) and Succubus (females for males). These are sexual demons who come to people at night in their dreams. Many people who suffer from these sort of sexual predatory dreams, have opened themselves up via pornography.

People are not "possessed" but become sexually oppressed by these sort of demons. What Christians need to know is that these demons do not all of a sudden come upon a person. The person has been exposing themselves to pornography for a while and get to the point where they seem to "welcome" these sexually explicit dreams. What can happen is that the demons start manifesting themselves even when the person is awake and become apparent even in their "day dreaming".

Even though the person is not "possessed" they become strongly oppressed to the point that they do not know how to escape from these entities who seem to hold so much control over the person via lust and its hedonistic unhealthy sexual passion.

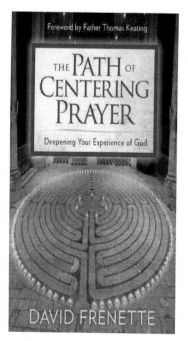

Drugs – Drugs alter the state of the mind and can totally open the doors of the mind to demonic activity. In fact, the Greek word for "sorcery" that we find in the scriptures Galatians 4:20; Revelation 9:21; 18:23 is pharmakeia. This is the same word that we get the word "Pharmacy" from. It is this sort of "witchcraft" that promotes the loss of control of the mind as well as denying the ability for the Holy Spirit to help us stay "soberminded."

False Religions and the use of New Age (pagan) Techniques – This is one area that has totally crept into the church today via a number of "wolves in sheep's clothing" teaching and promoting these things. These people claim to be Christians, but they themselves are completely deceived or are fully aware of what they are doing and purposely misguide the church by introducing these false and pagan ideas into the church. Some of these practices employ one or a number of the following…

- Emptying the mind
- Centering prayer
- Repeating a single word or phrase for long periods
- Walking the Labyrinth and using one of the these methods
- Slow monotone chanting or the use of "breath prayer"

These are just a few, and there are many more things that are seeping in. All these pagan practices have been introduced into the church and all of these open people's minds up to an altered state of consciousness. This is turn, opens the door to the mind and to the demonic and evil.

What we must remember is that Lucifer and his minions can easily appear as an "angle of light" and deceive people. These are all practices that can induce an altered state of consciousness. It's this altered state that can promote the loss of personal control of your mind.

Cursed / Hexed By Those Who Follow The Enemy – Many Christians do not believe that this can happen, they think that curses, hexes, magic and such are just biblical fables. They think that since "they" do not believe in them, they do not exist. But these "soldiers" operating in the spiritual are real and these things do work.

I personally believe that Tracye and I have had a lot of this put against us when we lived in Central America. So yes, there are people involved in occult activity in other countries and they will curse you and your family. This is how these people fight the spiritual war that we as Christians know so well is real, and this is where living a righteous life and wearing the armor daily will help protect you.

It's not that you can actually be cursed as a Christian, but rather those who are against Christ and his people can focus demonic activity on you.

The key to all of this is recognizing what is going on, and then start fighting against it. But since so many Christians don't even recognize what is going on, they have no idea how they can fight this oppression in the first place.

Check Your Home For Evil – Do you have things in your home that would allow demons and evil spirits access to you and your family? Are there tarot cards, new age crystals, inappropriate pictures, books, demonic music, collectables, and toys. Basically, anything that would allow the demonic to gain access into your home?

If there are things in your home, you may not see them at first. Ask God to help reveal to you the things that are evil and are acting as gateways into your life and your home. It might be something that you have had for a very long time that you have had no idea is acting as a portal into your life. This is why seeking God's help is important.

Once you have discovered these things, get rid of them. Throw them out and believe me, doing this will be very hard, but you have to do this in order to "cleanse your home" of things that bring in demonic oppression. In some cases, you may need to literally burn them. If God is prompting you to do this, be obedient and do it.

Do a Check Up From The Neck Up – Take the time to look at your life and ask God to reveal any areas that are opening up these gateways / portals into your life and your home. Are you watching the wrong kind of TV shows? Are they shows that deal with death, the demonic, the supernatural, magic and the spiritual? Basically, over all evil in the show? Do you listen to music that is demonically inspired? Are you involved in some sort of occult / pagan practice? Do you have anything in your life that promotes and exalts evil? Are you involved in drugs, pornography or other things that open your mind up to demonic oppression?

If you are involved in anything like the above, you need to seek God's forgiveness and confess your involvement in these things as sin. Then you need to seek God's covering to help you. I personally use holy anointing oil and anoint myself. Oil represents the Holy Spirit. Please know that the oil is not special, it is an act of faith to apply the oil that is special. You are crying out to God for protection and the oil helps one understand the covering of the Holy Spirit in one's life.

Check With Your Family and Friends To Make Sure They Are Not Bringing In Things or Exposing You To Demonic Oppression – Ok, so now you got your life together and you've worked to elevate the things in your life that can open doors for demonic oppression.

But… your life and home still do not "feel" right. There is a chance that others around you are bringing in things, watching the wrong shows, listening to the wrong music, involving themselves in some form of occult or pagan practices and now you have items around the home that create gateways / portals.

In some situations, you can help control these things and get them out of your home. But in other cases, when your spouse or older children refuse, then you have to pray God's protection over the situation and pray that God will intervene with what is going on. This is a true battle and you MUST make sure you are "prayed up", that you are wearing the full armor of God, and not just wearing the armor, but completely aware that you are wearing it and in the middle of the battle.

Like it or not, you need to become very spiritually aware. Anointing your home with holy anointing oil and banishing the evil from your home can work, but this is just a temporary fix if others are bringing in the evil (I will talk more about this later on in the book).

See, the demonic cannot come in unless they are invited or find some sort of portal or gateway. Praying over your home helps and will give peace for a season, but in the long run you are dealing with friends and family. If it is a friend that is exposing you and you have prayed and prayed for them and there is no change, then as hard as it is limit the time you are involved with this friend.

If it is family, then praying for them and praying over them is all that you can do. You can't kick out your spouse or child, but you can have a very strong influence in their lives. So much, that through your influence, prayer, and supplication to the Lord, their lives will begin to change. Again, we need to remember that we are fighting a spiritual war.

Conclusion

What we need to remember is that we are Christians bought with and cleansed by the blood of Jesus. We are indwelt with the Holy Spirit; thus God literally lives within us. Sometimes we need to look over our homes and our lives to make sure we are living a right life in these last days. There might be sins in our lives that we may not remember and finally God brings some of these past issues to light. Then we need to deal with them and seek out God's forgiveness. It is some of these past issues that may have opened these gateways / portals to the demonic and is causing the oppression.

When God does reveal these things, ask Him to help name a specific so that you can stop right then and there. Pray, repent and confess these past issues to the Lord. Ask Him to close these parts of your life and not allow the enemy access to you through this kind of spiritual gateway.

Finally, anoint yourself with holy anointing oil and ask God's mercy, protection, and favor in your life. Again, holy oil is just a tool that helps. There is something about anointing yourself and your home that God approves of. It seems to help strengthen your prayers because you are doing something in faith in Him. Another thing is to pray "out loud" so that the evil hears and will obey when you take authority in the name of Jesus. (More on this in Chapter 7)

We need to remember that "greater is He that is in YOU, than he that is in the world." (1 John 4:4)

Chapter 3 - To Many Snakes To Count

Since I have been openly working with deliverance, I have been getting a lot of emails from people asking some great questions.

One thing that I do notice is that the enemy is really hammering Christians today.

One of the most asked questions / statements is something like this ...

> *"I know that I have a demon problem. I have been praying and praying. I rebuke the enemy, bind it and cast it out. But nothing changes, I am still hearing the voices, still being tormented and under such heaviness, depression, sadness and at times I think I am going crazy.*
>
> *What am I doing wrong? Please help me! I am barely hanging on and completely exhausted with this battle. "*

I get emails like this quite often.

This is why I say that the enemy is hammering Christians in these last days that we are living in.

What is the problem that so many people are facing?

They are literally infested with demons. I mean they have a HUGE problem with hundreds of demons, as well as the minions that follow.

Snakes & You Living On The Fifty Yard Line

If this is how you feel, then work with me for a few moments.

Close your eyes and imagine yourself standing in the middle of a football stadium and you are on the fifty-yard line and you are the only one in the stadium.

Can you see that in your mind?

Now, draw a circle around where you are standing, say 5 feet in diameter.

Do you see yourself standing in that circle, on the fifty-yard line in the middle of a football stadium?

Now, I want you to imagine the ground is covered with rattlesnakes… hundreds, possibly thousands of rattlesnakes. They are rattling their tails, they are striking the air trying to bite you. In your hand is a flaming torch, you keep waving it at the snakes that are all around you. Some of them catch fire as you swing your torch, but 20 more moves in on you and your 5 foot circle is slowly shrinking and more and more snakes are getting closer and closer.

You are feeling some of them bite you and crawl on your feet. You keep swinging your torch and you continue to light some of the snakes on fire, but it isn't helping.

You are outnumbered and overwhelmed. Although there are too many to deal with, you keep fighting. They are wearing you down, biting you, and poisoning you. The pain, the hurt, and the hopelessness is becoming too much to bare.

To those of you who are reading this and have this problem, did I describe your problem pretty well?

You know that you are doing everything right, but the problem is that you are severely outnumbered.

AND…That is what demons do.

They ambush and overwhelm you. The next moment you realize that you are completely infested with demons that surround you. The voices won't stop. The pain in your heart is horrible. You just want it to stop, but they are rushing in on you and you are drowning in the voices, the thoughts and the horrible emotions.

Whosoever Shall Call…

Joel 2:32 "And it shall come to pass, that whosoever shall call on the name of the LORD shall be delivered.

James 4:7 "Submit yourselves therefore to God. Resist the devil, and he will flee from you."

When you are in this state, surrounded, outnumbered, panic and anxieties is so strong that it feels like boulders crushing you.

What do you do?

"Whosoever shall call" … this is a statement and promise that God gives us just for those times. All of a sudden, the fear and panic is now facing the great white throne of God.

SUDDENLY, your head breaks through the water's surface and you take in that breath of life that only God can give.

SNAP… some of those chains that were holding you down break away and fall off you. You feel a lightness come over you and bathe you in the Holy Spirit's warmth.

Your circle just got bigger. Instead of 5 feet in diameter, you now have 15-20 feet in diameter. But you still have the problem of all the snakes surrounding you and getting closer and closer. Now granted, they are not coming in as fast as before, but they are still coming closer and closer.

Does all this sound familiar?

OK, maybe it isn't snakes. No matter what, you are still being attacked from all angles and you're so overwhelmed that you don't know what to do. Your mind just stops thinking and you want to curl up into the fetal position.

You are demonized. You are literally infested with demons and you need deliverance.

Now the weird thing is that most people won't seek out deliverance. The main reason is that they don't know that deliverance is available.

All they have to do is call upon the Lord and He will deliver them.

But it never comes to mind.

So, they go through life unhappy, miserable, and lacking the joy that God promises because the demons steal every moment of any joy, peace, and happiness they might have.

Look or feel familiar?

What's The Answer?

Pouring your heart out to the Lord, crying out to HIM like you have never cried out before. Submit yourself to the Lord, resist the devil and he will flee.

But submitting means submitting your all, not 50%, 75% or 95%.

You must submit your "all". This is something that many Christians won't do.

It is almost as if they would rather live with the pain and torment, than submitting 100% of themselves to the Lord so that they can be truly free.

Kind of like a spiritual form of Stockholm Syndrome.

Yes, things are bad, really bad. The snakes are all over them, but some Christians would rather choose the snakes / demons instead of submitting to God.

Then there are some that say they will and they do it, but then they slowly drop their guard and demons covertly pour back in. One day they wake up and they are infested again with a horde of demons.

But then there are those who reach deep down inside themselves for one more battle, one more fight and at the speed of light deliverance comes.

There is power in the name of Jesus… to break every chain.

Suddenly there is VICTORY like never felt before.

THEY ARE FREE! THEY ARE FINALLY FREE!

They fall to their knees and thank God with all their hearts.

They then stand back up a changed person. They have just been through the unimaginable battle and through Jesus Christ they are victorious.

With sword in hand they draw that line in the sand and say NEVER AGAIN SATAN!

For those of you who stood up and continue to stand today, I give you this…

NEVER AGAIN SATAN!

Never again will I allow Satan to control my life!

Never again will Pharaoh (Satan) control me, because I have been delivered from his power!

Never again will I be a slave to Satan, I am now a Servant Warrior of the King of Kings, Jesus Christ!

Never again will I allow the devil to do what he desires in my life, I will resist the devil, and he WILL flee from me! (James 4:7)

Never again will I listen to or believe the lies of the devil, he is a liar and the father of lies! (John 8:44)

Never again will I listen to the voices of the wicked one!

Never again will I be vexed by unclean spirits! (Luke 6:18)

Never again will I be harassed by the enemy! (Matthew 9:36)

NEVER AGAIN!

Chapter 4 - My Deliverance Did Not Stick? Why?

I have been helping a number of people with the deliverance process. Helping them get rid of their demons. Many of these people do not realize that they are "demonized" or another way of looking at it is they have a "demon infestation" problem.

What many people do not understand, especially if they have gone to some sort of "deliverance crusade" or saw some person who is in town for his / her "deliverance seminar", that deliverance is an ongoing process.

Odds are when they have been to one of these events, many believe that their demon problem is over. For many it's a relief to have gotten rid of so much pain, darkness, and torment.

However, it's important to understand that when you are in the deliverance process, you are in a sensitive / fragile state. Based on my experience, what I am calling the "deliverance process", is about 90 days.

If you are truly working my program, you should see a change and start feeling "normal" again around week two or three.

It is at that time you will become a "newly cleaned house" this is the term that Christ used.

Being a "newly cleaned house" you are susceptible to the demonic because you have not put good habits in place to counteract the attacks that the enemy will throw at you.

If you think all your demons are gone, great.

**BUT know this, once you have been "demonized / infested"
YOU will always be a target to the enemy.**

What you need to ensure is that you don't return to those bad habits or situations that allow more doors to the enemy to be opened.

Scripture says …

> Luke 11:24 When the unclean spirit is gone out of a man, he walketh through dry places, seeking rest; and finding none, he saith, I will return unto my house whence I came out.

> 25 And when he cometh, he findeth it swept and garnished.

> 26 Then goeth he, and taketh to him seven other spirits more wicked than himself; and they enter in, and dwell there: and the last state of that man is worse than the first.

As we can see from this scripture, we need to understand and realize that deliverance is an on-going process of intervention, changing habits, and seeking Christ in all things.

Jesus warns that leaving a house clean, but unfilled with the Holy Spirit and the Word of God, will leave a person vulnerable to spiritual attacks and possibly encounter much worse consequences if not constantly attended.

Now this constant attention or what I call "Spiritual Situation Awareness" is challenging in the beginning because it means being vigilant and watchful against the enemy.

> 1 Peter 5:8 "Be sober, be vigilant; because your adversary the devil, as a roaring lion, walketh about, seeking whom he may devour:"

In Proverbs we read …

Proverbs 4:23 "Above all else, guard your heart, for everything you do flows from it."

One of the biggest complaints I hear from people who have gone through some sort of public deliverance is "It didn't work, I felt good for a month or two and now I am back in the same hurtful, dark, depressing place."

I often ask if that person worked on their deliverance process. Did the place they sought deliverance give them some sort of plan to help them keep the enemy at bay while in this fragile state of "strengthening their house"?

Often, they say no. They thought once it's done, they were good to go and can now go about life like nothing happened.

Then, it's like nothing ever happened and they are back where they were… major demon infestation all over again.

God's Word says that we should not allow things into our lives that are sinful, and that we should guard our hearts against such things that would compromise our walk.

Romans 12:2 "And be not conformed to this world: but be ye transformed by the renewing of your mind, that ye may prove what is that good, and acceptable, and perfect, will of God." We have a responsibility to respond and to seek after the things of God so our temples will be filled and the doors of our heart well-guarded.

Garbage in Garbage Out

There are countless doors that if left open, will allow attacks from the enemy. The obvious ones are easy, but the subtle ones are often the ones that leave you vulnerable.

-**Media and Entertainment** – this one is a major motivator. Music, TV, movies, internet, magazines, etc. Feeding your heart and mind the wrong things can end up leaving a tasty snack for a hungry enemy.

-**Sexual impurity** – Lust, fornication, masturbation and imaginations can leave wide open the door to vulnerability and a late-night treat for an enemy feeling "snackish".

-Toxic people – People who tether themselves to you, that keep you burdened down, that are obsessive or abusive. Everyone knows at least one person in their lives that hang up the buffet sign to the devil's delight.

There are many other areas of life, from temptations, exposures, or flat out rebellion that the enemy can feed off of. Allowing any access garbage, in any corner of your life, can lead to feeding the demonic influences in your life and allowing your temple to become ruined.

What Can We Do

Renew your mind –

> Ephesians 4:22-23 - 22 That ye put off concerning the former conversation the old man, which is corrupt according to the deceitful lusts;
>
> 23 And be renewed in the spirit of your mind;

In your early days of deliverance this requires deliberate and intentional acts of will to strain forward towards Christ. You will be getting attacked, so you will need to guard against this. The more we stay in His ways, the more our mind is refreshed and restored. We become renewed and less likely to fall into the snares that feed the enemy.

You have to be willing to let go of ALL your sin, you cannot keep a few things in your life that feel comfortable or familiar if it's going to be feeding the demonic influences.
No closet feeding.

Guard our hearts-

Withdrawing from places, habits or people, whose toxicity will allow the demonic to feed off of, is a must if we want to fill our lives with Christ. Leaving no room for the devil to get a foot hold.

When the Bible talks about the "enemy walking about like a lion, seeking whom he may devour", you better know he has an appetite that will never be satisfied until he can drag you through hell and to hell.

Put on the full Armor of God-

> Ephesians 6:11 – 17 – 11 Put on the whole armour of God, that ye may be able to stand against the wiles of the devil.
>
> 12 For we wrestle not against flesh and blood, but against principalities, against powers, against the rulers of the darkness of this world, against spiritual wickedness in high [places].

13 Wherefore take unto you the whole armour of God that ye may be able to withstand in the evil day, and having done all, to stand.

14 Stand therefore, having your loins girt about with truth, and having on the breastplate of righteousness;

15 And your feet shod with the preparation of the gospel of peace;

16 Above all, taking the shield of faith, wherewith ye shall be able to quench all the fiery darts of the wicked.

17 And take the helmet of salvation, and the sword of the Spirit, which is the word of God:
People tell me that they take on and off the armor of God. I ask, why ever take it off in the first place.

Why expose yourself to the enemy's attack when we do not have to? Wearing the armor takes practice and using spiritual muscles too.

Here is a little story that some of you may have heard before:

Back in my college days I used to be involved with group that is called the SCA, also known as the Society for Creative Anachronism.

Those involved would role play as if they were living in the King Arthur days. They would wear armor of all sorts and go bash each other over the head with rattan swords.

What is interesting is that today, it is actually seen as an official form of martial art. Well, I was one of those guys who enjoyed beating each other senseless. Now to be honest I was getting beaten on more than I was beating on others.

At one of these events I happened upon one of the well-known "knights" and struck up a conversation. One thing led to another and he let me hang out with him for the weekend, kind of being his "squire".
In these circles this was seen as pretty cool, especially if your knight was well known. Mine was well known.

This guy was really into the SCA, he owned a complete set of full plate armor. In fact he built it himself and was actually world renown for his ancient armor work. Rumor had it that he even worked on some of the armor that is in the tower of London. Yep, he was that good.

Well, I got a chance to try on his armor. It was about 50-60 lbs. of steel wrapped all over my body from head to toe. Wow… it was pretty cool.

Now, this is what was interesting, here I am standing in his armor and he comes over and barely pushes me with his index finger.

I just about fell over backwards because I was not used to wearing so much weight let alone know how to fight in it. He laughed and kept me from falling over backwards.

In that short moment he taught me a very valuable lesson that still sticks with me today.

What I learned was that it was different for him because when he was out on the "battle field" he was running and jumping and hitting people with his sword, bashing people with his shield, going full bore. He was also often the winner of the tournaments and have been made "king" of the local SCA group several times. This is a very high position in the SCA and it also meant that you were a true warrior.

Me, it was all I could do to just to keep standing up.

So why could he run around in this armor and I barely was able to stand?

Several things.

1 – He literally wore his armor every day in one form or another, so it became a part of him.

2 – Because he and his armor were one, this "trained" his body. This in turn conditioned him and he was always ready for the fight.

I tell this story because the armor of God needs to be seen the same way. It is not something that you just "throw on" and then think you are going to go out and do battle.

You need to consciously train and live in the armor daily.

Why? When that evil day does come, you have done all that you can to train…and having done all, then stand and fight.

If we are not wearing the armor daily, how does our "spiritual muscles" strengthen? If we are not used to wearing it and the armor becomes like a second skin, how long will we last in battle when that evil day comes?

By not actively wearing the armor daily we will fail.

Conclusion:

By applying these steps, you can starve the enemy of the food they feed on, your emotional and spiritual garbage.

No garbage, no rats.

But you must hold on tight to Christ. You do this by renewing your mind, guarding your heart, and armoring up against the enemy. This is how we starve the enemy and live in the fullness of what God has for you.

Chapter 5 - The Hard Questions

This is the first step to deliverance. From this point on you can choose to either stay as you are, which the odds are that you are miserable and not truly happy, or we can work together, and you can truly have freedom from oppression, depression, and horrible influence of the demonic.

Below you will find my basic questions. Some of these are going to be rather blunt and very private in nature.

Please know this is just a start, there will probably be more questions that God will put in your mind that you will need to write down in your garbage list.

Please give as much detail as you can when you answer your questions. The devil is in the details and if we are going to uncover the demons, then the more detail you can give with each answer you will be amazed at the demons you uncover.

Know also that I WILL NOT JUDGE YOU, you may feel at times that I am as you are working your way through this manual, but I am not. What I will do, is present pretty hard truths and at times, it's hard for people to swallow the hard truth.

NOTE #1 - there will be times where I might ask some pretty private and invasive questions. Thing is, the more honest you are with me and yourself, the faster we can proceed and really work at the problems at hand.

Know this, you do have the power within you through Jesus Christ to see deliverance. I can help guide you through this manual, but we will have to work together as a team, and at times you may think me a flake or idiot because of the things I ask you to do, write down, think about, pray about, or actions you need to take.

BUT know this, time will show you that you are making headway, the key is to listen and do what I recommend in this manual.

The key… Stay Persistent - Stay Consistent.

PLEASE GIVE AS MUCH DETAIL AS YOU CAN AS YOU ANSWER EACH QUESTION. The more detail and background you give reveals the "garbage" that is often found in the back corners of the mind. Remember, the mind is the battleground and we need to clear it out of all the garbage.

Following this will help you and me examine and focus on each question instead of pulling it out of a dialog.

The Garbage Test – Self Analysis

Are you a born-again Christian? If so, when did you accept Christ as your personal savior?

_____

_____

_____

_____

Can you provide me with a brief testimony?

_____

_____

_____

_____

Have you fully submitted your life to the Lord 100%?

_____

_____

_____

_____

Have you ever been baptized? If so when / how long ago? _____

If needed are you willing to get baptized again? _____

What demons do you believe are currently infesting you?

_____

_____

_____

_____

Have you sought out forgiveness of your sins?

_____

_____

_____

_____

Have you renounced the sins you have committed?

_____

_____

_____

_____

Do you have you any transgressions, ill thoughts, and bad thoughts of anyone in your present or past? If so, who and what is the transgression you hold against them?

_____

_____

_____

_____

Do you currently have any drug or alcohol issues, problems addictions?

_____

_____

_____

Have you used any drugs or alcohol in your past? If so, what, how much and how often?

_____

_____

_____

Do you smoke? _____

Do you have any occult sins or ties?

_____

_____

_____

Do you have any New Age sins or ties?

_____

_____

_____

_____

Do you have any rock & roll, satanic media, entertainment sins or ties?

_____

_____

_____

_____

Do you have any yoga, meditation, labyrinth, pagan sins or ties?

_____

_____

_____

_____

Do you have any witchcraft sins or ties?

_____

_____

_____

_____

What, if any, hatred do you have to yourself or others?

_____

_____

_____

_____

Do you cut on yourself, bang your head or self-injure yourself just to help make the other pain go away? If so, what is it that you do, and what are the "triggers" that cause the bigger pain?

_____

_____

_____

_____

Do you hold any grudges against anyone from your past?

_____

_____

_____

What do you do in your free time?

_____

_____

_____

_____

What do you do for work? _____

Do you attend Church, if so, what denomination?

_____

_____

PRIVATE AND INTIMATE QUESTIONS -- Please understand that a good number of Christians are being attacked by what is called Incubus and Succubus demons. They are sexual demons that appear as males and females. They attack in the night and initiate sex with the host. These demons get very ugly, mean, and they are dangerous. Their ultimate goal is to see you die, usually by suicide. Please know that I do not say this to put fear in you, but to warn you that these are very serious demons and many times we do not know they are even present in our lives. This is why I need to ask some of these questions. Even if you are not being accosted by a sex demon, please answer these questions with as much detail as you can.

QUESTIONS - Please answer these questions with as much detail as you can.

Are you married? _____

Do you love your spouse? Give detail as to why or why not.

_____

_____

_____

_____

Have you ever cheated on your spouse? _____ If yes, give detail.

_____

_____

_____

Are you still intimate? _____ If no, give detail.

_____

_____

_____

_____

If so, how often are you intimate? _____

When you are intimate are your thoughts on other men / women or other sexual situations? If so, explain.

_____

_____

_____

_____

Do you have sexual thoughts about others besides your spouse? _____ If yes, give detail.

_____

_____

_____

_____

Do you have any sexual sins or ties? _____ If yes, give detail.

_____

_____

_____

_____

Do you have any porn sins or ties? _____ If yes, give detail.

_____

_____

_____

_____

Have you ever been to an adult porn store? _____ if yes, give detail.

_____

_____

_____

_____

Do you masturbate?_____

If so, how many times a week? _____

What do you imagine while you are masturbating? What is it, that helps you climax?

_____

_____

_____

_____

How sexually active have you been in your past and present?

_____

_____

_____

_____

Do you have any homosexual / lesbian, group sex, B&D, ritual sex sins or ties? _____
If yes, give detail.

_____

_____

_____

_____

Do you see, feel or hear demons at night?_____ If yes, give detail.

_____

_____

_____

_____

Do you have any sexual dreams with a mysterious person who then makes you have an orgasm?_____ If yes, give detail.

_____

_____

_____

_____

Have you ever been sexually abused or raped in the past by family or by someone you know?_____ If yes, give detail.

_____

_____

_____

_____

Any other sexual encounters, that you know of, that may be important in discovering your demon issues?

_____

_____

_____

_____

If you are single, are you sexually active? _____

How many partners have you had in your life? _____

Are you sexually active now? _____

If so, describe your current partner.

_____

_____

_____

_____

EXPERIENCING ACTUAL DEMON ACTIVITY IN THE HOME -- Look these over and let me know what you are experiencing and please give some detail after each situation so I can better understand your situation.

Seeing orbs or strange lights? _____ If yes, give detail.

_____

_____

_____

_____

Catching shadows or streaks out of the corner of your eye?_____ If yes, give detail.

_____

_____

_____

_____

Hearing knocking or footsteps?_____ If yes, give detail.

_____

_____

_____

_____

Hearing voices, breathing, growling, barking, pig-like noises, or hissing in your ear as you start to fall asleep?_____ If yes, give detail.

_____

_____

_____

_____

Strange smells like smoke, burnt moldy wood, badly burned pork, rotten eggs, sulfur, etc.? _____ If yes, give detail.

_____

_____

_____

_____

Items being moved around the house?_____ If yes, give detail.

_____

_____

_____

_____

Sleep Paralysis, sleep walking, Hypnic Jerk, false awakenings, being slapped or touched while sleeping?_____ If yes, give detail.

_____

_____

_____

_____

Intense sexual dreams that feel real?_____ If yes, give detail.

_____

_____

_____

_____

Climaxing during a sexual dream but finding no discharge? _____ If yes, give detail.

_____

_____

_____

_____

Waking up and seeing gray, black, or pale greenish/gray clouds about 1 foot in diameter? _____ If yes, give detail.

_____

_____

_____

_____

Chronic fatigue, headaches, depression. Generally feeling drained like something is sucking the life out of you? _____ If yes, give detail.

_____

_____

_____

_____

Pets appear to see things that you can't. In many cases the animal will interact with something or appear fearful? _____ If yes, give detail.

_____

_____

_____

_____

Bruises, round bruises on the inner thighs, scratches, rashes, or bite marks and no memory of how they got there? _____ If yes, give detail.

_____

_____

_____

_____

Feeling intensely agitated for no apparent reason? _____ If yes, give detail.

_____

_____

_____

_____

Intense, nearly uncontrollable sexual urges or outbursts of anger? _____ If yes, give detail.

_____

_____

_____

_____

Sinus or allergy issues. Small amounts of blood in sinus drainage? _____ If yes, give detail.

_____

_____

_____

_____

Ringing or buzzing in ears? _____ If yes, give detail.

_____

_____

_____

_____

A heaviness or depressing feeling in the home? _____ If yes, give detail.

_____

_____

_____

_____

You feel like you are constantly being watched? _____ If yes, give detail.

_____

_____

_____

Electronics malfunction. Lights flicker, light bulbs blow, etc.? _____ If yes, give detail.

_____

_____

_____

_____

You feel a sense of confusion. Thoughts that used to come quickly to you seem hampered. You feel as though your IQ has dropped. You are not as mentally sharp as you once were. _____ If yes, give detail.

_____

_____

_____

_____

Synchronicities keep occurring. You keep seeing specific numbers like 11:11 on the clock or other repeating numbers. _____ If yes, give detail.

_____

_____

_____

_____

You experience missing time. Hours have gone by and you have no idea how you got where you are. _____ If yes, give detail

_____

_____

_____

_____

Thanks for taking the time to answer these. Once you do, let me look them over, pray over them and I might have more questions for you. _____ If yes, give detail.

_____

This area is for extra notes to yourself that you may think of…

Chapter 6 - Take The Demon Test

I have had you take the self-analysis test. Now I need you to take the demon test. What is amazing is that odds are very good that you know the demons that are inside you. They speak to you in their voices and you hear them. Look this list over and write down all the demons that you believe are oppressing you, telling you lies in your mind.

Demons love to torment the mind and so many of us let them speak to us in our mind thinking this is normal. But it isn't. It is being attacked and oppressed by the demonic.

Put a check mark by each demon/feeling/voice you think you have.

By marking these down, you can see what you are dealing with and knowing the enemy is the first step to the battle plan.

Know this, that deliverance from this is possible. I will be writing more on this in following articles.

The primary demon areas are…

Murder
The Occult
Lust
Pride
Mental Health
Unforgiveness
Sickness
Different Kinds of Vices
False Religions

These 9 specific areas are some of the major areas that demons will try and target once they move in for an attack on someone. These are "games" that demons will try to play on us. These are real life-and-death games / snares / fiery darts. This is why the Bible tells us to always be sober, vigilant, and alert for any kind of demonic activity that could set in on us, or any of our closest loved ones.

1. Murder

   Murder _____
   Hate _____
   Rage _____
   Anger _____
   Violence _____
   Death _____
   Revenge _____
   Destruction _____
   Darkness _____
   Suicide _____
   Jealousy _____
   Sadism _____
   Fighting _____

2. The Occult

   Fortune-telling – of any kind such as palm reading, crystal ball gazing, numerology, or seeing psychics. _____
   Tarot Cards, Angel Cards _____
   Ouija Boards, Angel Boards, Automatic Writing _____
   Séances and any involvement with mediums or spiritualists. _____
   Astrology and any form of horoscopes _____
   I Ching _____
   Hypnotism _____
   Transcendental Meditation or any type of Far Eastern Meditation. _____
   Crystals _____
   Witchcraft _____
   Satanism _____
   Voodoo _____
   Channeling _____
   Reincarnation _____
   Astral Projection _____
   ESP _____
   Dungeons and Dragons – role-playing games. _____
   New Age Movement techniques and activities. _____
   Necromancy _____

3. Lust

Lust _____
Fornication _____
Adultery _____
Pornography _____
Transvestism _____
Transsexuality _____
Prostitution _____

4. Pride

Pride _____
Arrogance _____
Haughtiness _____
Rebellion _____
Blasphemy _____
Control, Domination _____
Possessiveness _____
Contention _____
Quarreling _____
Critical, Judgmental _____
Selfish _____
Narcissistic _____
Unbelief _____
Skepticism _____
Greed _____
Paranoia _____
Deceit _____
Mockery _____

5. Mental Health

Fear _____
Depression _____
Torment _____
Dread _____
Hopelessness _____
Despair _____
Insecurity _____
Paranoia _____
Suspicion _____
Distrust _____

Insecurity _____
Loneliness _____
Shyness _____
Discouragement _____
Passivity _____
Lying _____
Deceit _____
Antisocial _____
Compulsive neurotic behavior _____
Phobias _____
Madness _____
Insanity _____
Schizophrenia _____
Multiple Personalities _____
Hearing Voices _____
Mind Control _____

6. Unforgiveness

Unforgiveness _____
Bitterness _____
Jealousy _____
Resentment _____
Anger _____
Stubbornness _____
Envy _____
Hard-heartedness _____

7. Sickness

Spirit of Infirmity (any kind of disease or illness) _____
Death _____
Anorexia _____
Bulimia _____
Insomnia _____
Abnormal amounts of lethargy, sleepiness _____
Epilepsy _____
Gluttony _____

8. Different Kinds of Vices

Alcohol _____
Cocaine _____
Heroin _____

Meth _____
Marijuana _____
LSD _____
Anti-prescription drugs _____

9. False Religions

Islam _____
Jehovah's Witnesses _____
Mormonism _____
Hinduism _____
Buddhism _____
Confucianism _____
Shintoism _____
Sikhism _____
Jainism _____
Zoroastrianism _____
Spiritualism _____
Christian Science _____
Hare Krishna _____
Scientology _____
Kabbalah _____
Unification Church _____
Freemasonry _____
The Children of God _____
EST _____
Eckanar _____
The Forum _____
The Way International _____
Theosophy _____
Rosicrucianism _____
Atheism _____
Legalism _____

List all the demons you checked off the list above see what you are dealing with. Know that you can be delivered.

_____

_____

_____

_____

_____

_____

_____

_____

_____

_____

_____

Here is a great promise from our Lord…

Joel 2:32 And it shall come to pass, that whosoever shall call on the name of the LORD shall be delivered.

Chapter 7 - Identifying Your Demons and Your Garbage

You should have taken both your Garbage Test and your Demon Test.

Look back to the Garbage Test / self-analysis and look at your garbage.

Odds are the demons or "feelings" you associate with are in direct connection to the "garbage" they are feeding off.

The garbage test shows your garbage and the demon test shows you the demons you are probably dealing with.

What we need to do is deal with your garbage and once we start doing that, many times the demons will just leave because you are starving them out.

Get rid of the garbage and you get rid of the rats (demons).

Your Garbage List

Your garbage list is probably the most important part of the program that I have developed. It is here where you write down all the sins that come to your mind, even if you have asked forgiveness for them in the past. **If you are thinking of them, the enemy is using them to help create garbage that they can feed on.**

Giving yourself an honest analysis will be the hardest thing you will ever do. People can give advice and diagnose issues based on what they know, but **only you** can look at the places in your mind and heart that no one else can go.

When you are looking at your life, there are tethers and triggers that allow the demonic influences into your life. Some, you can name by the fruit (consequences) that comes from it.

But discovering most of the junk in your life that demons will feed on, will be the result of a brutally honest and ongoing self-assessment that you will need to give yourself. This is why I say that deliverance is not a sprint, but a marathon.

The temptation to hold onto areas of your life that breed the garbage demons feed on is most of the reasons deliverance fails.

There are challenges to overcoming addictions, habits and mindsets. If you are not willing to completely renew your mind, then you will leave open the doors to the enemy's influence.

There is also the very dangerous reality that you may "love your demons" more than you want to be free from them. If demons have your affection or acceptance, then you are leaving them more than enough grounds to stay and multiply.

In some cases, such as in sexual encounters or a long history of occult involvement, there can be dangerous tethers to the demonic that people are not willing to sever. They are willing to keep that which has been present, familiar or even comfortable at times, around because they cannot see life without them. They are afraid of either being alone or angering a presence that they have felt has been "benevolent".

When you get to the point that you would rather keep the demon satiated rather than be free, you are already in a most dangerous place. It is a place that will lead to death down the line. And make no mistake about it, the enemy wants to deceive you anyway they can to put you through hell and then take you there… to your death.

But how you battle this is by taking away the garbage the demons feed on.

How Do You Get Started With This?

- Write down all your sins and transgressions from the earliest time you can remember. Also, write down all the people that you may have harmed, hurt or transgressed against.

- Write down any "legal rights" the demons are using against you. I have provided a list at the bottom of this plan that, so you can look over the demons legal rights that they are using against you. These usually are what the voices are tempting you with and then become guilty of.

Demons cannot enter into a person's body without having some kind of legal permission and legal right to be able to do so. They need some kind of an entry point to be able to get in and attach to someone, and that entry point will be their door opener.

There are spiritual laws that are in operation in our world and even demons have to abide by these spiritual laws that have been set up God. The Bible tells us in Revelation 3:20 that Jesus Himself will stand before us and knock on our doors to see if we will be willing to open up that door and allow Him to come into our lives.

In order to have Jesus come into our lives, we first have to be willing to give Him our direct permission to be able to do so, as God will never force Himself on any of us. He will let us know when He will want to come into our lives and that He will always be knocking on our doors. But, we will be the ones who will decide whether or not we are willing to open up that door for Jesus to be able to come into our lives.

The reason being is that God has given each one of us a full free will and He will never violate the free will that He has given to each and every one of us.

It's the exact same way with demons. Demons cannot enter in on the inside of a person unless they do something specific on their end that will open up the door for them to be able to come into them. And that something specific will be their legal right.

i.e. Masturbation - the voices tell you to do it, you do, and then you feel guilty. Break the legal right of masturbation, seek forgiveness and renounce it as "I will never do it again." At that moment the enemy does not have legal right over you in that area. They must leave as commanded by you.

Do this with all legal rights that the enemy may have over you.

NOTE -- You will sin and fail at times. Even Paul did. We all have our chinks in our armor. The flesh is weak, but the spirit is strong. At times we succumb to the flesh. Don't beat yourself up or think "it isn't working" if you fall from time to time. Just get back up again and rise above it.

Think of all the people who have hurt you, traumatized you, had sex with you, etc. Write them down, you probably have soul ties to these people that need to be broken.

Review your garbage test over and over again, take each somewhat negative item you have put down and really give it an examination.

- What sins have you committed?
- What transgressions have been committed against you?
- What transgressions have YOU committed against another?
- What legal rights have you given to the demons?

All of this is your garbage and you are not going to be able to write it all down in just one sitting. But if you work on this DAILY, you will begin to see deliverance and freedom from the enemy.

As time goes on, God is going to continue to reveal more and more "garbage" that you need to add to your list. I tell people to keep this manual with them always, that is, if it's possible. If it is not, you might want to get a small notebook to jot down "garbage" that God will reveal to you.

If you are still having trouble with this, think of our garbage like the many layers of an onion. You want to peel all of them back down to the very core. To help do that, ask yourself the following…

- Who
- What
- Where
- When
- How
- Why

I have provided a number of pages in this manual so that you can start writing down your garbage.

I want you to do it, here in this manual, so that you will have all these things in one place.

This way, you will not lose a journal, or misplace a steno notepad or such.

Write them and keep them here in this manual.

_____

_____

_____

_____

_____

_____

_____

PART 2

The Deliverance Processes

Battle Plan / Battle Preps

Chapter 8 - Demon Master Battle Plan

Here is my demon plan that I have put together for people such as yourself. This has been, and continues to be, successful with others I am working with and they have seen incredible victory.

The key to this plan is doing it EVERY DAY your first 2-3 weeks while you are in the first part of the deliverance process. Do not skip, do not slack, and do not give an excuse! Push through and stick to the plan daily no matter what.

IF YOU SKIP JUST ONE DAY, IT COULD SET YOU BACK TO THE VERY BEGINNING AND POSSIBLY EVEN BE WORSE.

It does not matter if you have done some of the things I mentioned in the past with this plan to fight the demons…. IF the plan tells you to do it, then do it again.

YOU MUST BE CONSISTENT AND PERSISTENT… This is the key to spiritual battle and you can't let up even for one day.

Now… once you are past the first 2-3 weeks and going into your 90 days of deliverance, you are in a very vulnerable place. Many people get overconfident and often stumble and fall. Some do not get back up and fight. They instead give into the old demons and they are often worse off than they were before.

If this happens to you, start your battle preps up again and work your garbage list. Write down what happened and what caused you to fall. Ask yourself, how did the demons take advantage of you?

Working Over Your Garbage List.

You should have at least a few things written down in your garbage list by now.

Write and work in your garbage list every night, or when you choose to do your quiet time. I usually suggest at night time, before you go to bed, because for most people that is when the enemy chooses to attack. At night when you are asleep.

This is part of what I call "Battle Preps" and I will talk more about that further on.

We will work from this list. It will probably take some time for you to do this. To ask God to bring forward in your mind, the things that you need to seek forgiveness of, and people you may have transgressed against.

Look over your list and pray. As you are looking it over, God may cause you to pause on a certain item on your list.

If He does, then pray over that item. Call out to the Lord and ask that He deliver you from this item.

Repent, Renounce and Break the legal right.

Do not rush this, think and really ponder each item on your list.

Pray 1 John 1:9 as you go over each item.

> "If we confess our sins, he is faithful and just to forgive us our sins, and to cleanse us from all unrighteousness."

A good idea is to also look up a corresponding verse that you can also pray for each item on your list.

Example - Masturbation = lust -- 2 Timothy 2:22 "Flee also youthful lusts: but follow righteousness, faith, charity, peace, with them that call on the Lord out of a pure heart."

EXAMPLE PRAYER

-=-=-=-=-=-=-=-==-=-=-=-=

Our Father which art in Heaven, hallowed be thy name. I come to you in the name of your son Jesus Christ and seek your forgiveness and deliverance. Please forgive me of _____ and know that I renounce this sin, and ask you to deliver me and keep me from temptation of _____.

Father I pray your word (bible verse here)

_____

Father in the name and blood of your son Jesus Christ I break any legal rights of
_____ at this moment.

Please bless me and make me holy as You are holy. I thank You and praise You for hearing my confession of sin and cleansing me from all unrighteousness.

Amen

=-=-=-=-=-=-=-=-=-=-=-=

I know that many people do not know the bible like one should. If you do not know bible verses, then here is another prayer breaking the legal rights that you can pray...

-=-=-=-=-=-=-=-=-=-=-=-=

Our Father which art in Heaven, hallowed be thy name. Please hear my prayer and command these demons out of me.... DEMON of _____ I break your legal right that you have over me, you no longer have that right nor my permission. You have no ground to stand upon any longer. I command you in the name and blood of Jesus Christ to leave me and I cast you at the feet of Jesus Christ and the white throne of God. "

-=-=-=-=-=-=-=-==-=--==-

You want to pray something like this over each of the sins that God has pointed out to you and you have written down in your garbage list.

Be humble and conscious of each sin and the prayer.

CRITICAL -- DO NOT make it something that "you have to rush through and get it done."

Each prayer needs to come from the heart, what you are doing in this process is "clearing out the garbage."

You clean out the garbage, and you will get rid of the rats / demons.

Chapter 9 - Tools For The Battle

1- Making Holy Anointing Oil For Spiritual Battle

Anointing oil is one of the key tools that I use in the deliverance process. There is also something special when one makes their own oil, specifically for their own personal use.

Can you go to the store and buy plain olive oil and use that? Yes, you can.

Can one go to a Christian bookstore and purchase anointing oil there? Again, yes you can.

But I find that when one prays over, excises and blesses their own anointing oil, it seems to help boost the faith of the individual where common store-bought oil does not produce the same effect.

I liken it to someone shooting a charging bear with a BB gun verses that of a 50 cal. machine gun. Both shoot, both hit, but one seems to do a much better job instead of the other.

Just so you know, there is no power in the oil itself, the power is in our faith, understanding and supplications unto God. That is where the power is. The oil is just a symbol or tool that we use to help focus our prayers.

This anointing oil is what I use in and on our home, personal items and property, but I also use it on myself and wear it as a fragrance or use it to anoint myself.

Here are the oils that I use…

Frankincense – http://amzn.to/2mj0foR

Myrrh – http://amzn.to/2n0OI7M

Cinnamon Bark - http://amzn.to/2m2GIjV

Cassia - http://amzn.to/2Az67I5

Patchouli - http://amzn.to/2qtVujG

Lavender – http://amzn.to/2miIo2t

Clove – http://amzn.to/2miIGGB

Jasmine – http://amzn.to/2n0EM8T

Orange – http://amzn.to/2mS4GuX

Cedar wood – http://amzn.to/2n0wiOQ

Rose – http://amzn.to/2nlKhvW

Feel free to use any oils that you wish to use. I also use a lite base oil like grape seed or sweet almond. You can use lite olive oil, but I do not use virgin or extra virgin because it will battle with the other fragrances. I then put my mixture in one-ounce bottles.

Base Oil, Grape Seed – http://amzn.to/2nlvkKp

Base Oil, Sweet Almond – http://amzn.to/2lTeh5e

1 oz. Amber Glass Bottles – http://amzn.to/2nlxM3u

Blending The Anointing Oil

This is where your own personal preference comes into play. I mix what I think smells good to me. But the one thing I make sure that I have is frankincense, myrrh, Cinnamon, Cassia and Patchouli oils, these are the oils mentioned in Exodus 30:22-25.

NOTE - Kaneh bosem, is one of the oils and many believe that it is either what is called "sweet reed" or Cannabis. Both are difficult to find, so I choose to substitute with Patchouli oil.

81

So, I have my base oils and then I will add to that my other oils and make an aroma that is pleasant to me.

I like lavender and clove because they have healing properties. They can help the healing process if you are using this oil on a sick child, or other family members.

To start, take one of your empty bottles and start dropping drops of the oils you have selected.

You can count your drops and write down your recipe if you want. Me? I tend to blend on the go and my anointing oil is never the same twice. But I do know the certain aroma that I do like and I have learned to mix and match my oils till I get that certain aroma.

IMPORTANT - While I am doing this, I am usually humming praise songs. I am also praying asking God to bless the oil, and to bless and protect everything that I anoint with this holy oil.

When you are praying over your oil, here is a prayer that you can use...

--=-=-=-=-=-=-=-=-=

"The Blessing of the Father Almighty be upon this item, and let all malignity and hindrance be cast forth hence from, and let all good enter herein, wherefore I bless thee and invoke thee. If there be any evil, be gone at this moment and use this item no more. Thank you, Father, for hearing my prayer in Christ Jesus our Lord and Savior - Amen"

=-=-=-=-=-=-=-=-=-

This is what makes this oil specific to you. YOU have prayed over your oil, asked God to bless it, asked God's favor when using it, as well as, ask God's protection when anointing against the enemy.

Why Do I Use It As A Fragrance?

By doing this, it helps me to reflect more on the Lord. I smell the sweet smell and it reminds me to think about the Lord, pray, praise, sing, etc. The fragrance helps me stay in a state of holy awareness, if that makes sense to you.

Often when I am at a speaking engagement I will anoint myself and the aroma helps me maintain a full-on mindset for the Lord.

For the women, I have seen some nice necklaces that are diffusers. Meaning that you can place drops of your oil on little porous stone balls and put them in a broach and you can smell the aroma all day.

For example, here is one that looks like a heart with a cross.

Heart Diffuser – http://amzn.to/2ITiKVC

In today's very busy world, we tend to not think about God all the time. Therefore, I like wearing my anointing oil. The key is to be able to use the aroma as a trigger to help you stay in a conscious state where we are thinking about the Lord all through the day. This in turn helps us to praise Him, thank Him and continue to talk to the Lord all day long. At least that is what it does for me.

2 - Audible Bible Playing In The Background

We know that when Satan was tempting Christ, His response was the Word of God, The Bible. This is why it is important that you have God's Word playing in the background. Now, you don't have to have this playing loud, just low enough so that it is barely audible will be fine. I recommend that you keep this playing 24 hours a day.

Why? Because the enemy hates hearing the Word of God.

By playing this in the background, I have found that it pushes the enemy back and weakens it. Demons do not like God's Word, so they seem to shy away when they hear the bible being spoken audibly.

I am a huge fan of Alexander Scourby reading the King James Bible. You can purchase the audio bible on CD here -- http://amzn.to/2nHik3G

If you do not have a small CD player (boombox / stereo) get one that you can move room to room. Play the CD's all the time, even when you are not home. You don't have to play it loud, just low enough that you can barely hear it in the background.

What About Praise & Worship Music?

I have noticed that playing praise and worship music benefits more **YOU** the person, vs keeping demons away. Demons HATE God's Word, but praise and worship music on its own, does not have much effect on them.

Do I encourage the playing of praise and worship? Very much so. It helps **YOU** keep in a proper state of mind and that is what is important. It also helps reinforce your deliverance process and even helps strengthen you as you are going through your deliverance process.

I highly encourage you to listen to praise and worship all the way through your deliverance process.

Here is a list of songs that I have put together on YouTube that you can listen to in the beginning, if you do not know of any songs to listen to. I add to this list often, so visit back and see what I have added.

LISTEN HERE -- **https://tinyurl.com/Battle-Preps-Motovation-Mix**

3 - Start Memorizing Scripture - Be Ready For The Attack

As I have mentioned how Christ dealt with Satan in the wilderness was by quoting scripture to him. Here are some good verses that you should memorize so that you have them in your head at all times.

James 4:7 "Submit yourselves therefore to God. Resist the devil, and he will flee from you."

Psalms 23

1 The LORD is my shepherd; I shall not want.

2 He maketh me to lie down in green pastures: he leadeth me beside the still waters.

3 He restoreth my soul: he leadeth me in the paths of righteousness for his name's sake.

4 Yea, though I walk through the valley of the shadow of death, I will fear no evil: for thou art with me; thy rod and thy staff they comfort me.

5 Thou preparest a table before me in the presence of mine enemies: thou anointest my head with oil; my cup runneth over.

6 Surely goodness and mercy shall follow me all the days of my life: and I will dwell in the house of the LORD forever.

1 John 1:9 "If we confess our sins, he is faithful and just to forgive us our sins, and to cleanse us from all unrighteousness."

1 John 4:4 "Ye are of God, little children, and have overcome them: because greater is he that is in you, than he that is in the world."

Joel 2:32 "And it shall come to pass, that whosoever shall call on the name of the LORD shall be delivered"

If the enemy is being persistent, then quote scripture out loud and it will make the demons go away also.

Chapter 10 - Daily Battle Preparations

This is the crux of the battle, your daily battle preparations, or what I call "Battle Preps."

The enemy does not like ceremony. It shows them that you are serious about your deliverance.

But the key in this, is that YOU MUST DO THIS DAILY.

Since the enemy likes to attack mostly at night, I have found that doing this in the evening is the best time, especially if you are dealing with an incubus / succubus demon (sex demon)

What battle preps are, is the preparing your mind, body, and soul to do battle. Again, the enemy seems to attack mostly at night, so we need to be ready for that attack and by doing our "battle preps" we are able to stave off a lot of the enemy attacks.

The Process of Battle Preps

1 - Shower - self baptize. While taking a shower, you want this time to focus on asking God forgiveness and to cleanse you from all unrighteousness (1 John 1:9). You are cleaning your body and cleaning your soul at the same time. Have the KJV bible or solemn worship music being played in the background while you are in the shower and as you are anointing yourself.

2 - Once out of the shower you must anoint yourself in oil. Place a few drops in your hands, rub them together and then rub it over the top of your head and down your hair. Anoint your heart / chest, anoint your hands / arms, and anoint your feet. Finally, if you are a woman dealing with an Incubus anoint your breasts and female parts front and back, this is where the demon is attacking, ask the Holy Spirit to protect you and protect / guard your sexual purity.

If you are a man and have a Succubus, then anoint the male parts front and back and as you are doing so, ask the Holy Spirit to protect you and protect / guard your sexual purity.

While you are doing the anointing process, you are praying and asking God's protection, favor, blessing, and that the Holy Spirit will guide you and direct you.

We read in scripture …

> 2 Samuel 12:20 Then David arose from the earth, and washed, and anointed himself, and changed his apparel, and came into the house of the LORD, and worshipped: then he came to his own house; and when he required, they set bread before him, and he did eat.

> Ezekiel 16:9 Then washed I thee with water; yea, I thoroughly washed away thy blood from thee, and I anointed thee with oil.

> Ruth 3:3 Wash thyself therefore, and anoint thee, and put thy raiment upon thee, and get thee down to the floor: but make not thyself known unto the man, until he shall have done eating and drinking.

3 – Spend time in prayer and review your "garbage list" and pray over some of the items you have written down.

4 - Spend time reading God's word out loud before you go to bed. You do not have to speak this loudly, but you need to speak it out loud.

Demons cannot read minds and they hate God's word. This is why there is power when you audibly speak God's Word, especially at night when you are getting ready to go to bed.

Remember, it is at night that the enemy likes to attack the most.

Continue daily, your battle preparations -- shower / self-baptism / cleansing, time with the Lord, washing self and soul. Anoint yourself once you get out, bless and consecrate yourself, thank and praise the Lord as you are anointing. Anointing oil represents the Holy Spirit and He is our teacher and protector. Conduct your quiet time with the Lord, read scripture, pray.

Continue daily to work over your Garbage List. The goal is to have all your items crossed out. But another thing is, that this is a long process and God will reveal to you things down the road that you will need to put on your Garbage List. When He does that, remember to add them to your list. This is why earlier I suggested a notepad. The enemy is great at distractions that cause us to forget. You want to make sure you remember the things that God puts on your mind.

The main key that you must remember is,
That you must be persistent and consistent.

The demons expect you to "give up" or "slack off" the moment you do, is when they will jump on you like white on rice.

By being persistent and consistent, you are not giving them the chance.

After a while this will become habit, but at first you need to be conscious of your thoughts and actions, and take action the moment the enemy pops its head up.

Dealing With The Demons - Spiritual Battle

First thing you need to know. You are dealing with an entity that is thousands of years old, but with the character of a 6 - 13 year old who is misbehaving in a big way, at least most of them.

You need to be stern and authoritative, just like you would to a young misbehaving child.

Do not "lose it" and yell at the demon. It brings you down to their level.

Righteous anger is ok, losing it and yelling isn't. I think you know the difference. If you understand that, then you know what you are dealing with and how you should act.

NEVER SHOW FEAR... They feed on fear and that's what they want, to feed upon your emotions.

STAY EMOTIONALLY PURE ... This is another area which they are feeding upon. You, your negative emotions, resentment, self-hate and loathing, etc. Every time you think on these things you are creating garbage that they are feeding upon. If you are dreaming it, try to wake up. If you are having sexual or other disturbing dreams, then take action. This is hard to do, but eventually your subconscious / Holy Spirit will wake you in your dream and you can take action.

STAY SEXUALLY PURE ... This is another area which they are feeding upon you. Try to wake up when you are having your sexual dreams and take action. This is hard to do, but eventually your subconscious / Holy Spirit will wake you in your dream and you can take action.

The steps that you need to take EVERY TIME, even when you suspect / think you are being attacked are as follows:

VERBALLY REBUKE - Tell it to stop & leave you alone. You recognize their attack.

VERBALLY BIND - Bind it, command it to stop by binding it. It does not have "legal right" over you and tell them that "You do not have legal right over me any longer. Jesus Christ, my Savior, took those keys back."

VERBALLY CAST OUT / AWAY – "I command you in the name and blood of Jesus Christ to go away, leave me alone, stop tormenting me, tempting me, etc. -- I cast you out of my home / myself / my presences and command you go and I cast you at the feet of Jesus Christ. Let Jesus deal with you... be gone now."

Demons do not read minds, so you need to verbally say it. If you are in a dream state, take action and verbalize in your dream. Don't think it, say it. This will take practice, but your subconscious / Holy Spirit will help you manifest this within you.

Quoting scripture at this point is also a good thing. I like James 4:7 and 1 John 4:4. Repeat them, over and over again, out loud. You will know when the enemy leaves you.

REMEMBER... you are dealing with a demonic infestation... you basically have hundreds if not thousands of rattlesnakes about you.

You are killing them off one by one.

SO, it will take a bit of time. But the more proactive you are and jumping on these things, the moment you notice an attack, the faster and quicker they will flee from you.

Chapter 11 – Identifying and Dealing With The Sexual Demons – A Special Address To Those Who Are Suffering This Sort of Attack

:::::: WARNING – Sexually Graphic Content Will Be Discussed ::::::

Demonic Sex – Incubus & Succubus, The Demons of Sex

The next two chapters are going to be graphic in its contents, so please be warned that I am going to be addressing issues that are very adult in nature.

Since the 1980's our nation has been suffering an ever downward sexual spiral. With the ability to have VHS, DVDs and now video on demand via the internet, we have immersed our nation in sex, but not only that, hard core sex.

As you know we have been out of the country now for over 4 years and upon returning one of the biggest things that I have noticed is there are more "adult stores" in main stream shopping malls. In fact, I was blown away to see an "Adam & Eve" store in an outside shopping mall next to other well-respected stores. This was not a small store either, but about the size of a regular apparel store or small sporting goods store.

Just driving down highway 6 here in the Houston area there are a number of these sort of stores all over.

This tells me one thing. The demand is high enough not only support this type of store, but competition is high enough that it is profitable for multiple stores to serve a rather small area.

Just in this area I have counted about 6+ adult stores in maybe a 7 – 10 mile radius.

If the demand was not there, then there would not be as many of these places. But what is amazing is that they are in shopping centers and malls. This means that they are no longer on the back streets and more Americans see this sort of store as "normal."

Another thing that I have noticed is that you see more women frequenting this sort of store. In fact, it looked like the Adam & Eve store catered more to women than men based on their window displays.

It seems that no matter where you turn, in America these days, there is some sort of sexual message being portrayed and / or promoted.
Why is this?

To be very honest, anything that drives a Christian to this is not from the individual alone. That individual is being influenced by a demon.

Now, that is not to say that the individual is not responsible, somehow they have opened up a door in their lives and allowed the spirit to have access to them. In a sense they have invited that spirit in knowingly or unknowingly.

See, we as Christians are free from the sins of the flesh, but like it or not, the flesh is strong and when you feed the flesh it becomes even stronger.

But in today's world there is a severe obsession with sex and I truly believe that this attitude is demonically influenced via the Incubus and Succubus demons.

What Are These Sort of Demons?

Incubus is a demon that is more "male" in their desires which means that they tend to attach themselves to women.

Succubus are demons that are more "female" in their desires which means that they attach themselves to men.

Now as I have mentioned in past articles, Christians are not able to be possessed by demons. They can though be influenced, oppressed & depressed, and even haunted.

I am going to be very bold here and this is something that does affect the church at large today. People who cannot control the urge to masturbate or watch, read, and think about pornography are being influenced by some sexual demon.

There are many Christians out there that are plagued with this problem, we see it in the news all the time. Even some pastors have been affected by these issues.

Addressing Women on This Issue

In addressing the sexual demon, I want to talk to the women first. So please know that I am not singling women out. What we need to remember is that women are more demonically influenced because they are the weaker vessel.

Another issue that I want to point out is that women are being targeted for the demonic sexual attack. A great example is the fact that in sex stores, female toys are prolific. If you go to some of these online stores, you will notice that there are more "toys" geared toward being used by women than there are being used by men. This is not a small business and the sex toy business earns over $15 billion a year.

Traditionally its men who are thought of in the western world as the sexual deviants and all, but when you look at what is being sold out there for sexual pleasure, a good 80% of sex toys and such are geared toward women more so than that of men.

FACT – When we imagine having sex in our minds and fantasizing mentally via masturbation, we are opening doors where were can actually summon a sexual spirit to help us manifest this thing we are imagining.

This is especially dangerous with women because women are more emotional and mentally stimulated. It is a fact that some woman can achieve an orgasm from thought alone.

Look at all the romance books that so many women are hooked on. The book "50 Shades of Grey" has led so many women astray, that they now have vivid sexual thoughts and are being lead down this sinful path.

It is these sort of thoughts and actions that open the doors to sexual spirits becoming attracted to that person.

Once a demon / spirit is attracted to you, there is a chance that it will then attach itself to your life and "haunt" you sexually.

Have You Experienced Some or All of The Following?

Do you have sexual thoughts out of the blue?

Are you drawn to pornography via reading books and articles? Most women experience pornography in the written form where men are more drawn to visual pornography. The reason is that women are more mentally driven where men are mostly visually driven.

Even if you are married, do you often fantasize or have sexual thoughts about men in your past or possibly some man you saw or know? No, you are not going to act on it in most cases but what we need to remember is that demons seek to steal, and destroy, that means attacking your marriage and your marriage bed.

If you are single, do you find yourself going from boyfriend to boyfriend? You give that person your body and in a month or so you are on to the next boyfriend? Later, you find that the sex just isn't good anymore and so therefore you must be "falling out of love" with this person? You jump to the next boyfriend and the sex is intense and yet it you keep following that same pattern.

Do you find fantasizing about these men and masturbating to be more fulfilling that the act of sex itself with these men?

Are you driven to masturbate even when you really don't want to? Are you being hit with such a strong urge to masturbate that you want have an orgasm just to give yourself some temporary relief?

Have you noticed that many of your orgasms are super intense when you are fantasizing about things you may have read, seen, or from men in your past?

Do you use sexual "toys" to help create an even more intense orgasm?

If you can answer yes to several or more of these questions, there is a chance that you have opened yourself up to the sexual demons and that possibly one has attached itself to you.

When you open yourself up like this, you are giving these demons access to your life. In turn these demons will cause guilt, shame, and even prevent you from having a pure and holy sexual relationship with your husband or soon to be husband.

When a demon has attached itself to you (still speaking to women here) they do not want you to have any solid relationships with any other man.

NOW, here is the interesting fact, many demons seek and drive women to have sexual relations with other women. Thus, the rise of lesbian relationships going on today.

These Incubus demons will do everything they can to drive all the good and decent men from your life. They will cause you to have huge amounts of guilt and shame. They tell you in one moment how sexy and desirable you are and then when you are driven to masturbate, they tell you how horrible you are. It is this sort of sexual roller coaster you become trapped in.

Here is a question, do you have sex dreams where you literally have orgasms? Odds are this dream person that you are having sex with in your dreams is an Incubus, a sexually driven demon.

Having a sexual demon attached to you is one of the hardest things to deal with.

Why?

You are driven by the sexual experience. It literally is a drug. When you have an orgasm, you are being shot up with endorphins, a hormone that makes you feel really good, happy, satisfied, etc. These experiences become habit forming and thus you move from maybe using your fingers to stimulate yourself to toys and then extreme toys. In other words, you are chasing the endorphin high and this is demonically influenced.

You literally have to stop the sexual habit and stop chasing after that sexual high. But it is the demon that influences you and has a strong power over you because you have opened yourself up to this spirit. They have the ability to bombard your mind with sexual thoughts If you have really opened yourself up, they literally have to ability to stimulate you physically as well.

This becomes a very powerful influence and the individual becomes trapped in this sin and becomes a sexual slave to the demon.

How do you break this?

You need to have a stronger influence in your life, and that is Jesus Christ. He is the one that can push these demons off of you, free you and keep you safe from these demonic attacks.

What You Need To Do

You need to repent of every sexual sin and deviant act you have done.

You must submit your life fully to Him and start living a right life in these last days.

You need to become accountable to yourself and to Christ.

You then need to destroy all those books, videos, toys, etc. that cause and help you to sin.

When you feel the urge rising up, you MUST recognize it as an attack from the enemy trying to tempt you. This is where memorizing scripture helps. I often recite Psalms 23 and have memorized it for when I am being attacked by the enemy.

> Psalms 23
> 1 The LORD is my shepherd; I shall not want.
> 2 He maketh me to lie down in green pastures: he leadeth me beside the still waters.
> 3 He restoreth my soul: he leadeth me in the paths of righteousness for his name's sake.
> 4 Yea, though I walk through the valley of the shadow of death, I will fear no evil: for thou art with me; thy rod and thy staff they comfort me.
> 5 Thou preparest a table before me in the presence of mine enemies: thou anointest my head with oil; my cup runneth over.
> 6 Surely goodness and mercy shall follow me all the days of my life: and I will dwell in the house of the LORD forever.

I recommend cleansing and anointing your home with holy oil. If you are married, you and your husband do this together. If you are single, then you pray over your home, or apartment yourself.

If you find that you have more sexual thoughts in the bedroom, anoint your bed and ask God's blessings on it. If you find yourself doing sexual things in the bathroom, then anoint the bathroom and shower.

Finally, you need to dawn the armor of God and learn to use it daily. The spiritual battle wages minute by minute, hour by hour, day by day.

Some days we will be attacked, other days we will not. But no matter what, we need to be ready for the attack, recognize the attack and use our Spiritual Sword, God's Word – The Bible, to fight back these attacks and that is where your nightly battle preps come into play.

Scripture says…

James 4:7 -Submit yourselves therefore to God. Resist the devil, and he will flee from you.

That is how we fight and continue to fight. We must resist the devil and not give him a foothold on our lives.

If you have any questions, please do not hesitate to contact me.

The enemy has the high ground, we have got to start fighting back and pushing back the enemy.

In the next chapter I will discuss the Succubus demon that attaches and attacks men.

Chapter 12 – Identifying and Dealing With The Sexual Demons – A Special Address To Those Who Are Suffering This Sort of Attack

:::::: WARNING – Sexually Graphic Content Will Be Discussed ::::::

Demonic Sex – Incubus & Succubus, The Demons of Sex

In the last chapter I addressed the women.

I wrote to the women first, not to single women out, but to point out that women are the weaker vessel and are more demonically influenced because they are the weaker vessel.

Today I want to address the men.

What Are These Sort of Sexual Demons?

First, as far as we know there are no specific genders when it comes to demons. They are spirits without form, so naturally they do not have the physical attributes that a male or female would have.

There are two types of sexual demons that are known.

First, an Incubus is a demon that is more "male" in their desires which means that they tend to attach themselves to women.

Second, Succubus are demons that are more "female" in their desires which means that they attach themselves to men.

As I have mentioned, Christians are not able to be possessed by demons. They can though be influenced, oppressed & depressed, and even haunted. It is this sort of sexual haunting that seems to be taking place in the world today.

I am going to be very bold here and say that this is something that does affect the church at large today. People who cannot control the urge to masturbate or watch, read, and think about sex are being influenced by some sexual demon.

There are many Christians out there that are plagued with this problem, we see it in the news all the time. Just look at all the pastors that have been affected and publicly humiliated and their preaching career destroyed. In these cases, we clearly see that the demon was successful in destroying the pastor, upset the church and in many cases destroyed the marriage.

This is why I am writing this series on demons as a whole so that when we are being attacked, we can recognize the fact and then take the proper action to resist and push back the enemy. This is a serious topic and much of the church does not have knowledge because in many cases it isn't even being taught.

Because of this lack of teaching, many people do not understand that they are being demonically influenced. It has become too easy to blame the day to day chaotic hustle and bustle in the world.

Another issue is that because this is not being talked about or taught in churches today, demons, angels, and the spirit realm, are often thought of being part of a fairy tale, not real, imaginary.

This line of thought is very dangerous and can cause great harm to those who think like this and yet are being tormented by the very demons they think are part of the fairy tale stories.

I say this because most men tend to think logically and not emotionally. It is easy for men not to believe that they are being influenced by demons and figure that it is just them or strike it up to the world's woes. This is why it is dangerous.

Addressing Men on This Issue

I know that this is a tough topic because of a number of reasons…

1 – Men are macho and there is that whole "machismo" thing going on. "Hey, I'm Joe Cool and the women just dig me."

2 – Male pride as in "Hey, I can handle this, I know what I am doing, and I can stop anytime."

3 – Sex is being pushed down our throats at every turn. You cannot avoid the sexy billboards on the road, 80% of the ads on TV, and an even higher number when it comes to magazines. The world pushes women to dress very provocatively and many do. Sex is in our face most of the hours that we are awake and if we have a demon influencing us, then it is there when we sleep as well.

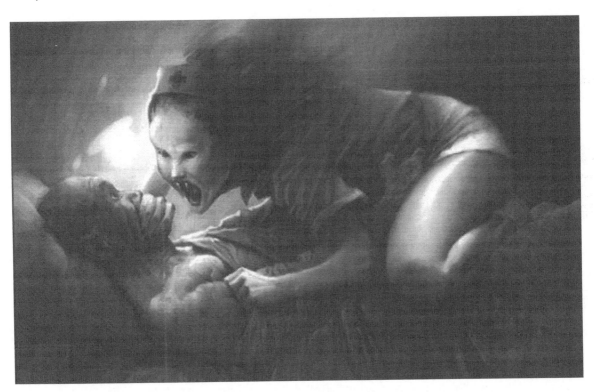

4 – With the dawn of the internet, sex behind the computer screen has risen to astronomical amounts. Access to the plethora of sex online is as easy as a few key strokes and wham bam it is there on your screen.

Because men are so visually stimulated it is easy to see why so many men have trouble in this area.

But what many men do not realize, is that through sexual pleasure, we open up conduits, doorways, and portals for demons to influence our minds both awake and asleep. Thus influencing our lives and our marriages.

Do You Have Sexual Demons Influencing & Haunting You?

Do you …

Watch porn online?

Do you have a stash of porn magazines in your home?

Do you frequent porn shops and those sex arcade booths that show videos?

Do you have very strong urges that pop into your mind and out of the blue to masturbate?

Do you frequent strip clubs or some of these sports bars where the waitresses have very little on in the way of clothing? I.e. Hooters, Twin Peaks, etc.

Do you visit some of the online chat rooms where you and some other person (women or man) talk about hot and heavy sex while you or both of you masturbate?

Do you hire or frequent the services of prostitutes?

If you partake in any or all of these, then there is a very good chance that you have fallen prey to a succubus demon and they have a stronghold on you.

Listen, because men are so visually driven, any sort of voyeurism that drives you sexually means that you have a succubus attached to you, especially if you are being driven to homosexual acts or mental images.

Demons are driven to do one thing that is steal, destroy, and kill and if they can take any pleasure while doing that, they will. Their sole purpose in being a succubus is to live out their own sexual perversions by entrapping men. They then drag men down a horrible path of sexual deviancy that in turn causes shame, guilt, and confusion which in turn becomes the trap.

In one moment the demon is tempting the individual to be sexually deviant and then in the next moment when the male submits, they are then condemning that male, quilting them at being a weakling and some perverted fool.

To those of you who are suffering, how often have you heard something like this?

"How can YOU be a Christian when you are there lusting and masturbating to porn? Obviously, you are not man enough for your wife. How can you call yourself a Christian when you are some sexual pervert?"

This becomes a horrible sexual roller coaster and turns into a sexual addiction. Not that sex in and of itself is addictive, but it is the endorphins that one becomes addicted to.

See, endorphins are a substance formed within the body that naturally relieve pain. They literally have a similar chemical structure to that of morphine. So, the result is that they help stop pain, bring on happiness and produce a soothing happy and pleasurable mood. In other words, it creates a sexual high during sexual climax.

In a Godly relationship between a man and a woman it's these endorphin experiences that actually cause and reinforce the couple's bond and as scripture states "become one flesh".

But when one is involved with a demonically driven sexual relationship, then it is all about self, self-pleasure and chasing after that sexual endorphin rush that a climax produces. But like any other drug, the "high" weakens and the person has to get stronger doses to achieve the same "rush."

For the person who is chasing after the sexual high, particularly for men, that means watching a higher form of a hard-core movie or looking at even more explicit sexual images, getting weirder and weirder and going deeper into deviant sex so that one can get that same sexually charged climax high.

God created sex to be good between a husband and wife and it's a beautiful thing. But satanically driven sex is not of God. It is purely selfish and will ultimately destroy a marriage. This is why we need to remember that a demon's job is to steal, destroy, and kill.

They are real and if you are suffering from the symptoms that I have talked about here, then you need to face the fact that you are being haunted by a succubus demon and they will destroy your life.

Here is a hard fact… when you are involved in all forms of sexual deviation, adultery, homosexuality, bisexuality, as well as an array of other hedonistic lusts and perversion, you are making yourself to look like a powerful lighthouse in the dark that will eventually attract these sexually driven demons.

For your information, in many cases it isn't just one demon, when there is a strong sexual host that demons can prey upon, they come in droves. Just look at the man who was possessed by "Legion" there were many demons infesting and inhabiting this single man.

What You Need To Do

First and foremost, you need to repent of every sexual sin and deviant act you have done. You must submit your life fully to Him and start living a right life in these last days.

You need to become accountable to yourself and to Christ. Learn to walk the "servant warrior" walk, by doing what is right in the eyes of the Lord.

You then need to destroy all the books, videos, toys, etc. that cause and help you to sin. When you feel the urge rising up, you MUST recognize it as an attack from the enemy trying to tempt you. This is where memorizing scripture helps. I often recite Psalms 23 and have memorized it for when I am being attacked by the enemy.

> Psalms 23
> 1 The LORD is my shepherd; I shall not want.
> 2 He maketh me to lie down in green pastures: he leadeth me beside the still waters.
> 3 He restoreth my soul: he leadeth me in the paths of righteousness for his name's sake.
> 4 Yea, though I walk through the valley of the shadow of death, I will fear no evil: for thou art with me; thy rod and thy staff they comfort me.
> 5 Thou preparest a table before me in the presence of mine enemies: thou anointest my head with oil; my cup runneth over.
> 6 Surely goodness and mercy shall follow me all the days of my life: and I will dwell in the house of the LORD forever.

Finally, I recommend cleansing and anointing your home in holy oil. I am assuming that you are married and if you are, do this together. If you are single, then you pray over your home or apartment yourself. If things continue, then you may need to get your pastor, elders and other mature Christians come to your home and pray for your home as well.

If you find that you have more sexual thoughts in the bedroom, anoint your bed and ask God's blessings on it. If you find yourself doing sexual things in the bathroom, then anoint the bathroom and shower.

Finally, you need to dawn the armor of God and learn to use it daily. The spiritual battle wages minute by minute, hour by hour, day by day.

Some days we will be attacked, other days we will not. But no matter what, we need to be ready for the attack, recognize the attack and use our Spiritual Sword, God's Word – The Bible, to fight back these attacks.

Scripture says…

James 4:7 -Submit yourselves therefore to God. Resist the devil, and he will flee from you.

That is how we fight and continue to fight. We must resist the devil and not give him a foothold on our lives.

If you have any questions, please do not hesitate to contact me.

I hope that this article has helped someone out there.

The enemy has the high ground, we have got to start fighting back and pushing back the enemy.

Consider joining my Servant Warrior Group on Facebook. There you will meet others who know the battles you have been through.

Do you want to be part of the Servant Warrior Special Forces?

Check out our group on Facebook @ - https://www.facebook.com/groups/theservantwarrior/

Part 3

The Long Term Battle

Chapter 13 – Fighting The Battle Long Term Basic Training

God's Word states …

1 Peter 1:16 because it is written, Be ye holy; for I am holy.

This is a challenging thing to do, but if we submit to God's help and direction, we can slowly over time grow more and more like Him and less like the world.

IF you are reading this battle manual, then what will eventually take place is that you will rise and become a Servant Warrior. This is what I call those of us who have been through the demonic wars and have overcome through the blood of Jesus Christ our Savior.

We need to remember that once we have been demonized, we have a target on our backs and therefore we learn to take that "higher path" forsaking all others, picking up your cross and following Him.

That is why I say "there are a lot of people out there that claim this, but in reality, there's really not that many." A lot of people give lip service, but rarely do most people back it up by really living it out.
Many try and fail. But believe it or not failure is a good thing. It is what you do after you fail that strengthens the metal with of which you are made.

Those who do choose to take the action, and to really live this idea out, they / you are the ones who become The Servant Warriors.

When you choose to walk the servant warrior path, you become the superior person as opposed to that person who has their life set to "autopilot" just drifting down the river of life allowing life to take them wherever. You have been through spiritual battles that others cannot understand. But more than that, you have fought and have won. You know what the enemy looks like close up and personal. You have taken them on and have won.

Now, I know there are some of you out there who is reading this saying "how dare I call myself superior."

Like it or not, it is the superior person who tries harder and takes the right path verses the one of least resistance. We must, for if we slip, we know what demons are waiting for us in our old mundane lives that we once lived.

The superior person chooses the ways of the Lord verses what they "believe" or "feel" what is right.

It is also the servant warrior who is more aware of the enemy inside because they battle with that enemy daily.

To use a modern term, that enemy is called "Despicable Me."

In scripture it is called "The Flesh" and you know what? Your flesh wants to ruin your life. That is why I call that part of me "Despicable Me."

See the average Christian today really does not understand that their flesh will NEVER seek the ways of the Lord.

As I have said, most people bend to their flesh and compromise themselves. Why? Because it is the easy thing to do, it is the easy way out.

Look at how many are out there that basically convey the idea of ..."Who cares! I have my fire insurance, I am saved by grace, so I can sin like hell."

Now, do most people proclaim it that way, in a "in your face" sort of statement? No, not at all.

But like it or not, that's basically how the average "autopilot" Christian lives their life.

Look at Playboy? Sure, why not? I am

saved by grace.

Go out and get drunk on Friday night? Sure, why not? I am saved by grace.

Smoke that joint? Sure, why not? I am saved by grace.

Check out that cute mail boy or secretary at work, undressing them in your imagination? Sure, why not? I am saved by grace.

Get what I am saying?

The Servant Warrior works hard to not allow these things to come into play. He or she does not give sin that foot hold.

At least 95% of the time.

But there are those times when "Despicable Me" wins out, and when "Despicable Me" does, regret, shame, and guilt come into play and it feels horrible.

I know that when my "Despicable Me" wins, I feel worse than worse. My heart is heavy, I have a knot in the middle of my stomach. I am not walking with that pep in my step. I feel like the world has dumped every bad thing it can across my shoulders and I am collapsing under the weight.

It seems that you will never feel free of this oppressive state.

And you won't, that is, until you do one thing.

>   1 John 1:9 -If we confess our sins, he is faithful and just to forgive us our sins, and to cleanse us from all unrighteousness.

See, until you make that true commitment to serving Christ, one will continue to live that life of ups and downs constantly being rocked to and fro.

It is our sins, our "Despicable Me", that constantly keeps winning and it seems like we are never free of all the destructive sins.

People plead and beg God to take those pet sins away, but they keep having a grasp on us.
"Despicable Me" is strong and most people think that "Despicable Me" will just go away.
We pray, we fast, we do all kinds of things, and as much as I hate to say it, it does not matter.
"Despicable Me" will always be there.

Why?

I am going to let you in on a little secret. "Despicable Me" AKA your flesh is in a war against you.

Your flesh will constantly attack you. If it isn't from one direction, it's from another.

Something else, remember that line a long time ago "The Devil Made Me Do It? "

Hog wash.

It was your flesh battling against you, yourself, and I. AND.... YOU LET YOUR FLESH WIN. See the moment you let up, your flesh finds that foothold and will start hacking away at you till you are living a life of regret, shame, guilt, spiraling out of control till you finally crash and burn.

Paul stated it this way...

> Romans 7:18 -For I know that in me (that is, in my flesh,) dwelleth no good thing: for to will is present with me; but how to perform that which is good I find not.
>
> Galatians 5: 17, 19-21 -For the flesh lusteth against the Spirit, and the Spirit against the flesh: and these are contrary the one to the other: so that ye cannot do the things that ye would.
>
> 19 -Now the works of the flesh are manifest, which are these; Adultery, fornication, uncleanness, lasciviousness,
>
> 20 -Idolatry, witchcraft, hatred, variance, emulations, wrath, strife, seditions, heresies,
>
> 21 -Envyings, murders, drunkenness, revellings, and such like: of the which I tell you before, as I have also told you in time past, that they which do such things shall not inherit the kingdom of God.

Here is some inside information. "Despicable Me" desires to participate in adultery, fornication, idolatry, hatred, strife and drunkenness."

Now some of you may be saying "Not my flesh Ray"

"Oh yes, your flesh!"

It does not matter who you are your flesh is hell-bent on dominating your spirit.

What makes the Servant Warrior different? The servant warrior does not accept defeat. The true servant warrior will ultimately rise up using the word of God (The Sword) and make the flesh obey.

The common autopilot Christian has no idea what to do.

See the common autopilot Christian doesn't care that they sin. Remember, they have their fire insurance, so they are "saved by grace, and can sin like hell."

If it feels good, they do it.

How To Fight The Flesh / "Despicable Me" – Basic Training

Listen, I am going to be honest. Being a servant warrior DOES NOT make us immune against the battles, what it does is give us the courage to stand and fight. We as servant warriors learn to use the tools, weapons and ideals that we learn from God's Word to battle "Despicable Me".

Basic Training Point #1 – Bring your Flesh / "Despicable Me" into subjection

1 Corinthians 9:27 -but I keep under my body, and bring it into subjection: lest that by any means, when I have preached to others, I myself should be a castaway.

It other words Paul is saying that we need to bring our bodies into submission. When we just let our bodies, thoughts, emotions, etc. get the best of us, The Flesh / "Despicable Me wins.

When we bring our bodies into submission, then we, the "servant warrior" keeps the things of the flesh at bay.

This is a daily struggle for all of us and for some it is a minute by minute struggle. But no matter what, it is a struggle. How we win is by being in God's Word – The Sword.

The more we know and use our sword, the more we can fight the battles against The Flesh / "Despicable Me."

Basic Training Point #2 – Make No Provision For Your Flesh

Romans 13:14 -But put ye on the Lord Jesus Christ, and make not provision for the flesh, to fulfil the lusts thereof.

To provide provision means to give food and comfort.

So, what do we do? We do not feed the flesh. We do not give it what it desires. We do not comfort it.

We starve it so that it is weak.

Guys, stop looking at those scantily clad women. Women, you stop looking at those "beefcake" guys. Stop hanging out at the magazine section of the bookstore peeking at Playboy, Playgirl, Maxim and Cosmopolitan.

Stop hanging out with people who like to go to the bars and get drunk on Friday nights. Stop watching those shows that promote sex, drugs, and lascivious behavior. You know what you should and should not watch. Grow some courage and turn off the filth. There is an old saying "GIGO" = Garbage In – Garbage Out.

Start saying NO to The Flesh / "Despicable Me" and YES to the spirit feeding the Servant Warrior in all of us.

We do this by being in His Word, living with it, memorizing it, and training with it. It is our spiritual sword and unless we train, we will be useless when The Flesh / "Despicable Me" decides to take action against us and ambush us when we are at our weakest.

Basic Training Point #3 – Mortify Your Flesh

Colossians 3:5 -Mortify therefore your members which are upon the earth; fornication, uncleanness, inordinate affection, evil concupiscence, and covetousness, which is idolatry:

What does Mortify mean? It means abstaining to the point of "putting to death" the action or undesired behavior.

Once you starve something it becomes weak. When you completely abstain from the sin, that sin begins to wither away. Now it will never go away, but when you completely abstain from feeding that sin, it is like it shrivels up and is no longer active.

NOW… just because it is shriveled up it doesn't mean it's gone. You feed that sin and it will come back with a vengeance.

So now that you are not feeding the sin and giving it comfort, you can start abstaining from the sin which in turn causes the sin to become seriously weak and ill effective for The Flesh / "Despicable Me" to use.

But again, the danger is thinking you can feed the sin here and there, cautiously keeping it at bay.

See, sin does one thing and one thing only. It kills.

How many of you are going to get into a cage with a live tiger? Sin is the same thing. Like a tiger it will sense when you are not looking or at a disadvantage. It is then that it will pounce on your and rip you to shreds.

Sin when you are playing that game of feeding it here and there it does the same thing. By toying around with it, occasionally feeding it, one day it will pounce on you. Even though that sin is in a weakened state, it is still dangerous like the tiger. Like the tiger, it can pounce on you when you are not paying attention, or you are distracted, or not training with the sword when you should be. Whatever the excuse or reason, it will pounce. When it does, it will take you down because you yourself are in a weakened state and you have been feeding the sin and not knowing that it is getting stronger again.

This is why we are called to "mortify" the flesh. Abstain from all of it. Not entertain it at all what-so-ever.

Basic Training Point #4 – Walk in the Spirit

Galatians 5:16 -This I say then, Walk in the Spirit, and ye shall not fulfil the lust of the flesh.

See when we bring our bodies into submission, we do not feed or give comfort to the sin, we mortify / abstain from everything dealing with the sin, we can then start walking in the spirit.

When we walk in the spirit, The Flesh / "Despicable Me" cannot take a foothold in our lives. Its ability to temp and do evil is greatly diminished. Again, that sin is not gone, but it is pushed back so far in the back corner that it does not have any influence with us. That is unless we start dabbling in the sin again, looking upon it, feeding it, and paying attention to it, etc., etc.

Which by that time we are no longer walking in the spirit, The Flesh / "Despicable Me" is winning and the internal battle is rearing to start up again.

The key is to not stop walking in the spirit. Stay on the path of righteousness and continue to do the right thing in the eyes of the Lord which whom we serve.

Basic Training Point #5 – Crucify Your Flesh

Galatians 5:24 -And they that are Christ's have crucified the flesh with the affections and lusts.

Once we have gotten this far in our basic training. We can say that we are walking the Servant Warrior Path.

We have put our flesh to death. We no longer desire it, we no longer feed it, comfort it or long for it. We have in a sense "crucified" our flesh and instead of serving the Flesh / "Despicable Me" we now serve Jesus Christ, The King of Kings and Lord of Lords.

But this is just the beginning. In many of the martial arts you have a ranking system. The beginner is the "white belt" and the advanced is the "black belt."

See, once the practitioner of that fighting system goes through all the ranks it does not mean he or she has learned all there is to learn. No, it means that they now have all the foundational basics. Now that they have the black belt, the real training starts taking place.

The same goes here.

This is not the ending point, this is just the beginning of the training. In the next installment of this series, I want to take you through "Advanced Training" so that you can fight the flesh even better and truly live a right life in these last days that we are living.

By doing that, we will truly be great Servant Warriors and be able to do the Lord's work without hesitation, and boldly "Go Ye Therefore" standing for the Lord and proclaiming the gospel to the world.

Chapter 14 – Fighting The Battle Long Term Advanced Training

In this chapter, it is my goal to take you past the basics and really help you cement with advanced battle training that you can take with you for all your life.

Long Term Advanced Battle Training

Last chapter I talked about how we can fight the flesh and the ways of the world.

I called that part "Basic Training."

For a quick review, we covered the following talking points…

Basic Training Point #1 – Bring your Flesh / "Despicable Me" into subjection

Basic Training Point #2 – Make No Provision for Your Flesh

Basic Training Point #3 – Mortify Your Flesh

Basic Training Point #4 – Walk in the Spirit

Basic Training Point #5 – Crucify Your Flesh

Now that we have the basics out of the way, now the real training begins.

With the "basic training" we brought "The Flesh" under some semblance of control. If we do not continue to not feed, mortify and crucify the flesh daily, then The Flesh / "Despicable Me" will rise up again and we will be "sinning like hell" and have to fight this horrible fight all over again.

Now, is living a life of constant internal battles a great thing? No not at all. It is a horrible way to live and it is absolute misery.

But if we continue to go back to "The Flesh" then we will continue to have these struggles.

To prevent these internal battles with "The Flesh" from taking place, we need to get into the advanced servant warrior training and that means take some serious action.

To win the war against The Flesh / "Despicable Me", one needs to realize what it is, and that is a true battle. That means down and dirty fighting. The Flesh / "Despicable Me" is not going to let up. It will continue to fight daily. That is until you really learn how to tame The Flesh / "Despicable Me."

Like in a real war battle, the side that rapidly overwhelms the other side will usually win. The more firepower, the more ammunition you must hurl at The Flesh / "Despicable Me" the more it will cause the enemy to fall back.

Remember the term "Shock & Awe"? That is what you do. But instead of using real world bullets, bombers and cannons, we use scripture, prayer, & praise.

When you feel The Flesh / "Despicable Me" starting to wiggle a little, it's wondering if you are paying attention, that is when you pounce and give them all you got.

Bam... You give it the scripture you have memorized.

Wham... You pray asking for God's Help.

Boom ... You praise God for the victory.

If you do this at the very first sign of The Flesh / "Despicable Me" coming to life, you will win the battle.

So what do you need to maintain this state of vigilance against The Flesh / "Despicable Me"?

Advanced Training Point #1 – Sever All Bad Influences

Psalm 1:1 -Blessed is the man that walketh not in the counsel of the ungodly, nor standeth in the way of sinners, nor sitteth in the seat of the scornful.

1 Corinthians 15:33 -Be not deceived: evil communications corrupt good manners.

You don't hang out with people who condone drug use, pornography, hedonism, drunkenness, theft, revelry, lawlessness, etc., etc.

I am going to be very blunt with you. You do not give people like this any of your time. You do not look to understand who and why they are. You do not negotiate, compromise, or have any dealings with them.

IF YOU DO… they will help reawaken The Flesh / "Despicable Me". They will work to coerce you, tempt you, lead you astray, seduce, pull, just about anything they can do to cause you to fall away from God.

This is why you sever all bad influences. This especially means those are living the C.I.N.O life (Christian In Name Only).

Is this hard? You betcha. That is why this is "Advanced Servant Warrior Training" and not the basics. You are going to have to knuckle down and get serious.

Do you truly want to be a servant warrior or not?

Now, I can hear some of you say, "Well Jesus hung out with sinners."

Yes, He did. In fact, He was surrounded by them 24 / 7 because everyone is a sinner. What makes Jesus different is that He is God in the Flesh. None of us can claim that.

We are here to be ambassadors to the world on behalf of our Lord and Savior. That does not mean that we freely partake of the world. We are to be light. Light shines and illuminates. It does not get in the fray and get dirty.

See, when you play in the devil's playground, you ALWAYS get dirty.

How you prevent this is by not getting in there in the first place.

We as Servant Warriors are called to a higher purpose, and NOT allowing the devil any foothold in your life from any source that would bring us down and off the path of the Servant Warrior.

Advanced Training Point #2 – Set No Wicked Things Before Your Eyes

As I have written in the past I used to be a smoker of Cigars & Cigarettes. This is something that God convicted me of, so to me, it is a sin. But I will not walk up to someone who smokes and call them a sinner. I will tell them the harm that smoking causes, and those who are Christians should not damage the temple God gave us.

I say that because the first step to sin is looking upon it.

> Genesis 3:6 -And when the woman saw that the tree was good for food, and that it was pleasant to the eyes, and a tree to be desired to make one wise, she took of the fruit thereof, and did eat, and gave also unto her husband with her; and he did eat. 7 And the eyes of them both were opened, and they knew that they were naked; and they sewed fig leaves together and made themselves aprons.

The devil is cunning and knows how to cause us to stumble. The first step Eve took to sin was to look upon the fruit.

This is why when we are in a store that sells cigars and such, I don't even look in that direction. Why put that temptation in my mind? You prevent doing that by not even looking.
If your Flesh / "Despicable Me" likes getting drunk of Friday nights. Stop looking at booze.

If your Flesh / "Despicable Me" likes sexy women and porn, don't oogle the women at work, or in the store or on TV. Avert your eyes and look somewhere else.

Same goes for women. If your Flesh / "Despicable Me" likes those sexy guys and plants sinful thoughts in your mind. Stop looking and avert your eyes.

> Psalm 101:3 -I will set no wicked thing before mine eyes: I hate the work of them that turn aside; it shall not cleave to me.

Advanced Training Point #3 – Take Heed To What You Hear

> Mark 4:24 -And he said unto them, Take heed what ye hear: with what measure ye mete, it shall be measured to you: and unto you that hear shall more be given.

Have you heard the music today? I mean it is utter filth. Most of it talks about having sex on a whim with whomever you are with. Swearing, cussing, killing, pro-theft, anti-Christian, anti-morals, and anti-family. Defiling and degrading one's self and women in one way or another.

If you could create movies just on pure lyrics alone, you would be amazed at the filth that you would see.

That is what most music today is made up of, filth, perversion, hedonism, and the list goes on.

Advanced Training Point #4 – Command Your Flesh / "Despicable Me" with Authority

Galatians 5:24 -And they that are Christ's have crucified the flesh with the affections and lusts.

Here Paul talks about "crucifying" your flesh. When you're Flesh / "Despicable Me" starts to rise, you do exactly like Christ did when tempted. You use the Word of God to slay the temptation.

Christ, when he was being tempted, did not use is own strength. Every response that he gave to Satan, was from the Bible (Old Testament). He used God's Word to defeat temptation.

See, when you speak to your flesh with the Word of God, it can do nothing but retreat. The flesh and the spirit cannot coincide together. Remember Basic Training Point #4 – Walk In The Spirit? As long as you remain in the spirit, the flesh will not gain a foothold. That means praying all the time, listening to proper music, listen to the audio bible, watch proper TV shows, etc., etc.

Advanced Training Point #5 – Take Authority Over Your Mind

Romans 12:2 -And be not conformed to this world: but be ye transformed by the renewing of your mind, that ye may prove what is that good, and acceptable, and perfect, will of God.

By renewing our mind, thinking and working to memorize scripture, singing songs of praise and edification to God, thinking on Him and His Word, these are ways that we renew our minds.

It is through this sort of "immersion" that we constantly grow and learn more about God. Again, the flesh and the spirit cannot coincide. So the more you meditate on God, the less room is given the Flesh / "Despicable Me" to gain a foothold.

Advanced Training Point #6 – Flee From Temptations Of The Flesh

Genesis 39:7 -13 And it came to pass after these things, that his master's wife cast her eyes upon Joseph; and she said, Lie with me.

8 But he refused, and said unto his master's wife, Behold, my master wotteth not what is with me in the house, and he hath committed all that he hath to my hand;

9 There is none greater in this house than I; neither hath he kept back anything from me but thee, because thou art his wife: how then can I do this great wickedness, and sin against God?

10 And it came to pass, as she spake to Joseph day by day, that he hearkened not unto her, to lie by her, or to be with her.

11 And it came to pass about this time, that Joseph went into the house to do his business; and there was none of the men of the house there within.
12 And she caught him by his garment, saying, Lie with me: and he left his garment in her hand, and fled, and got him out.

13 And it came to pass, when she saw that he had left his garment in her hand, and was fled forth,

As I have said before. If you play in the Devil's playground, you will get dirty.

You cannot play, flirt or dilly dally with sin and not come out without a scratch. Sin does one thing and one thing only, it kills.

When you are confronted with temptations of the flesh be it sexual, financial, drink, food, or other, you can do one thing and one thing only, turn 180 degrees and run as fast away as you can.

There are no other options.

Now some of you may be asking… "Food"?

What was the first thing Adam & Eve was tempted with?

Yes, the enemy even uses food. It is funny how often we forget that one.

So, when you are faced with temptation, FLEE!

Advanced Training Point #7 – Surround Yourself With Fellow Servant Warriors

Proverbs 27:17 Iron sharpeneth iron; so a man sharpeneth the countenance of his friend.

This is one of my favorite Servant Warrior verses. As Servant Warriors, the main goal is accountability. We are to be accountable to God, our family, our friends and finally ourselves.

By surrounding ourselves with other Servant Warriors, we will be able to maintain our stand.

These are people like you and me. They too have fought the demonic battles and have had victory. It is through fellow brothers and sisters who have fought the good fight where we can gain a different strength. No more do we feel alone, now we have another person who knows what it is like to fight the battles of the night, to cry out the name of Jesus and the demons flee. It is this sort of victory that only other Servant Warriors know.

I am reminded of a man named Hur and Aaron who accompanied Moses to the top of a hill to watch Joshua fight the Amalekites. As long as Moses had his hands held up, the Israelites were winning the battle. After a while Moses' arms started to droop due to fatigue. Hur and Aaron jumped in like true Servant Warriors and helped their friend Moses to hold up his arms and because if that, the Israelites won the war.

Aaron and Hur were there when Moses needed them most.

You want other servant warriors around you so that they can hold you accountable and that you can hold them accountable. You want to be able to reach out and support as well as be supported. It is my hope through our ministry and this Battle Manual that more and more Servant Warriors will come and join our Special Forces.

Do you want to be part of the Servant Warrior Special Forces?

Check out our group on Facebook @ - https://www.facebook.com/groups/theservantwarrior/

There are no "Lone Rangers", in fact The Lone Ranger had Tonto to hold him accountable.

We must do the same thing. Have fellow Servant Warriors we can be accountable to.

Battling your Flesh / "Despicable Me" is the tough part of walking the Servant Warrior life. It is something that you have to work at daily and continue to grow.

I am starting a special email list for those who wish to challenge themselves to be Servant Warriors. If you wish to be on that list, email me and I will add you.

Finally, never give up, keep pushing forward.

> 1 Corinthians 9:24 -Know ye not that they which run in a race run all, but one receiveth the prize? So run, that ye may obtain.

I know that this is hard, believe me, I know. I deal with these same issues. In fact, we read that even Paul dealt with his own "thorn in his side." We all have them, but we will win in the end. Our goal is not perfection, our goal is to submit to God so that HE can change us from the inside out.

We are just clay in the master's hands.

By submitting and living a right life in these last days, we will become more subtle in His hands and easier to work.

If you have any questions, please do not hesitate to contact me.

Chapter 15 – Putting Specialized Battle Plans in Place

You have done a great job on your deliverance, you are free and serving the Lord in great ways.

All of a sudden, a thought comes into your head, be it sexual, immoral, hateful, some wrong thought, much like the thoughts that the demons would put in your brain when they were oppressing you.

What you need to recognize is that this is an attack and you must go into the defense right away and push back the enemy.

But what do you do?

This is where have battle plans in place so that when you are attacked, you have a place to fall back to and defend yourself.

So how do you create and put together these battle plans when you don't even know how you are going to be attacked?

You look at your garbage list.

As I have said in earlier chapters, once you have been demonized, you will be a target for them for the rest of your life. This is why you have be situationally aware and by having said plans in place you will know what to do at a moment's notice.

It is your garbage list that will help you discover your "triggers" that will put you in places where you are vulnerable for attacks.

For example, it is pretty much expected of you to join the rest of the office staff for drinks at the pub down the street. Before you were having way to much like many of the others. You had this written down in your garbage list as one of the areas you needed to clean up so thus keep the booze demons away.

NOTE – I am not talking about an alcoholic in this situation.

You did not like getting ripped on those "office meetings" and it always bothered you, but on the flip side the voices in your head kept telling "oh have another one."

So, you did.

By looking at your garbage list as well as any other note you have about this certain area in your life, you want to look of ways to stop the "triggers" or things that will give the enemy cause to oppress or influence you.

Trigger – Going to the Friday night after work office meeting at the pub. Where you were really drinking A LOT.

Situation – Peer pressure at work these days are pretty hard. The ways of the world are pushed on us and it becomes a temptation to the flesh. BUT, you have witnessed how people who do not attend the after-work Friday business meetings are not progressing at work, getting the menial tasks, being passed over for advancement and such. AND walking around with a club soda in the hand is not office PC.

You need to be there and for the sake of your job you need to look like you are fitting in.

Battle Plan

1 – Nurse a long neck bottle of beer. You can even put water in it if you finish the beer. Brown bottle and no one knows the difference.

2 – If you are really being tempted, go to the bathroom and have verses on small business sized cards that you can read outload, pray, ect.

3 – Rebuke, Bind and Cast Out those thoughts who are trying to gain a foot hold.

James 4:7 Submit yourself to the Lord, Resist the devil and he will flee.

4 – Spend enough time there to get noticed and make the impression, but then leave say after an hour or so.

Now, this is just an example and I have had several of my people that I am working with face this sort of situation. This is roughly the battle plan we put in place. But what one has to do is when being faced by an attack by the enemy, work your battle plan.

Having a battle plan and not using it is dangerous and opening you up to re-infestation issues.

You are a "clean house" now. You need to keep it clean and protect it.

what you want to do is look over your list and put a plan together.

Name the following…

PROBLEM / TRIGGER

SITUATION

BATTLE PLAN

By writing down the Problem / Trigger you are able to look at it from a better vantage point and then see what the Situation really is.

Once you have a Situation and can name the Problem / Trigger, you can then come up with a way to defeat that situation by defeating and attacking or preventing the the problem / trigger to even get a foothold.

This will take a little bit of practice, but if you come up against one of your triggers / problems, do not go in thinking you can handle it without a plan in place.

Failing to plan is a plan for failure.

Thing is that when we fail, we possibly open doors to the demonic and then we are a real problem back on our hands again.

If you have problems grasping this idea. CONTACT ME at my website and use our Contact Form. We can schedule a time to chat on Facebook and I can possibly help you put together a battle plan for a situation.

Resources

Website – http://raygano.com

Email – ray.gano@raygano.com

You Tube Channel – https://www.youtube.com/c/raygano

Facebook Page - https://www.facebook.com/RayGano

Twitter - https://twitter.com/RayG_Prophezine

Patreon - https://www.patreon.com/raygano

You Tube Videos

Battle Preps Motivation Mix - https://tinyurl.com/Battle-Preps-Motovation-Mix

The Demonic Wars Videos - https://tinyurl.com/The-Demonic-Wars

Books

Deric Prince – They Shall Expel Demons: What You Need to Know about Demons - Your Invisible Enemies >> http://amzn.to/2E8ital

Deric Prince – Pulling Down Strongholds >> http://amzn.to/2BZnQmB

Karl Payne – Spiritual Warfare: Christians, Demonization and Deliverance >> http://amzn.to/2BdqNDf

Francis MacNutt - Deliverance from Evil Spirits: A Practical Manual >> http://amzn.to/2C101dY

Audio

Alexander Scourby reading the King James Bible. >> http://amzn.to/2nHik3G

Do You Need A Coach? I Am Here To Help

I am here to help you as you know, but if you don't follow the plan we have put in place, then you will constantly be taking 2 steps forward and 3 steps back.

How we do this is by staying in constant contact. I am on Facebook and I use the Facebook message system. I have this on my phone also, so I can get your messages just about anywhere I am.

Please friend me at -- https://www.facebook.com/RayGano

I do try to keep some semblance of hours that being 8:30 AM – 7:30 PM.

I am more than happy to help with any questions or support for 1 week.

If you wish to have more help and coaching, then you can get 1 month's support of unlimited questions. I have to charge for this because I am getting so many requests and so many questions from so many that I have to prioritize.

What I am offering is 1 Month of Battle Preps Support for $50.00

If you choose this I will also give you PZ Insider Access for 6 months to raygano.com which opens you up to our audio section as well as our entire deliverance section. You will also receive our 20+ page PZ Insider Report for 6 months delivered in PDF format to your email every Monday like clockwork.

YES.. I want 1 Month of Battle Prep Support -

https://tinyurl.com/1-Month-Battle-Preps-Support

Made in the USA
Middletown, DE
05 April 2018